1001 CYCLING TIPS

THE ESSENTIAL CYCLISTS' GUIDE

hannah reynolds

Vertebrate Publishing, Sheffield
www.v-publishing.co.uk

1001
CYCLING
TIPS
THE ESSENTIAL
CYCLISTS' GUIDE

hannah reynolds

First published in 2021 by Vertebrate Publishing.

 Vertebrate Publishing
Omega Court, 352 Cemetery Road, Sheffield S11 8FT, United Kingdom.
www.v-publishing.co.uk

A CIP catalogue record for this book is available from the British Library.

ISBN 978-1-83981-109-8 (Paperback)
ISBN 978-1-83981-110-4 (Ebook)

Front cover illustration © Julia Allum represented by www.meiklejohn.co.uk
All photography individually credited.

Design by Nathan Ryder, production by Cameron Bonser and Jane Beagley, Vertebrate Publishing.

Printed and bound in Europe by Latitude Press.

Vertebrate Publishing is committed to printing on paper from sustainable sources.

FSC
www.fsc.org

MIX
Paper from
responsible sources
FSC® C106600

contents

introduction

Even though I have written all these tips down, I can't take credit for the creation of more than a handful. These are all tips that have been passed on to me throughout my cycling life by people I have ridden with, talked cycling with or worked with. A mixture of club cyclists, amateur racers, old pros, new pros, physiologists, coaches, physiotherapists, bike guides and mechanics.

The cycling community is very generous with its advice. Just watch out, not all advice is good advice. There is a lot of received wisdom in cycling, and a fair amount of received nonsense too, that many of us like to follow as it is part of cycling culture. A good argument about sock length can kill at least an hour of a five-hour training ride.

If someone mentions following 'the rules' to you, ignore them, unless it directly relates to a race or event. No one can be disqualified from being a cyclist because their valves weren't at six o'clock in a photo or they have hairy legs. No one with a bike can be disqualified from being a cyclist, full stop.

When I started cycling, I was lucky enough to be taken under the wing of some very knowledgeable and patient riders who helped me navigate my way around common beginner errors, but some things can only be learnt through practice and experience. I've had my fair share of avoidable mechanicals, navigational errors, embarrassing kit choices and etiquette faux pas. I've blown-up, bonked, been caught out by the weather and been dropped on more rides than I can remember! Hopefully these tips will offer a few shortcuts, or life hacks, so that my mistakes can save you from doing the same.

I've almost certainly left out as many tips as I have included. I am sure there will be many that cause disagreement and there will be many alternative ways to arrive at the same solutions. I look forward to the debates! My most vital tip is to lean on the cycling community around you – it is a limitless source of friendship and advice.

Enjoy the ride!

acknowledgements

Thank you to the many people who have given me tips and advice through the years. A special mention to my former colleagues at *Cycling Weekly*, Norwood Paragon cycling club and the late Keith Butler, and my Evans Cycles teammates of the past. Thank you to John for all the cycling adventures; if it weren't for you, many of them wouldn't have happened!

feedback and updates

If you have any feedback or questions regarding this book, then please drop me a line:

hannah@hannahmreynolds.com

I'm also on twitter as *@HannahMReynolds*

For writing and public speaking assignments please visit *www.hannahmreynolds.com*; for the joys of cycling in France, and more on my guidebook *France en Velo*, visit *www.franceenvelo.cc*

Sarah Ross on the North Coast 500 in Scotland. © *Stephen Ross*

Cycling through Shedden Clough, Lancashire, England. © Joolze Dymond

Clowne Greenway, Derbyshire, England. © Rosie Edwards

001

BASICS (1–161)

'Cycling isn't a seasonal sport. You can ride all year round, provided that you have the right kit and the right attitude.'

Gravel biking into the Peak District from Sheffield, England. © *John Coefield*

BASICS (1-161)

CHOOSING A BIKE (1-23)

1. So, you want to be a cyclist? I could say something cheesy about cycling being a state of mind. But that would be nonsense. The only thing you need to be a cyclist is a bike.

2. When choosing a bike, the first thing to think about is not the bike, but you and your lifestyle.

3. Bike genres are getting increasingly niche and nuanced, and drilling down into the detail can be overwhelming, but it starts with identifying your needs.

4. Narrow down what you want to do with the bike, starting with the big questions. Visualise your bike ride – where are you and where are you going?

5. On-road or off-road? This sends you down two distinct paths (although hybrids and gravel bikes like to blur that boundary a bit).

6. Do you want to carry things on your bike? If you do, then it is time to explore bikes with racks or even cargo bikes.

7. If you are planning on riding off-road, how technical is the terrain you want to ride and how much do you enjoy technical challenges?

8. If you are planning to only ride on roads, are you after fast and light or convenience and comfort?

9. There is no such thing as a 'do it all' bike – every bike is better designed for some things than others. But you can get a bike that does most things OK. I'd put gravel bikes in this genre.

10. That said – there is nothing to stop you riding a heavy, full-suspension bike to the office; you will still get there fine, albeit a bit more slowly.

11. For some cyclists it *is* about the bike. They are the ones that say things like 'N+1', then won't come out on your ride because they don't have the right tyres for it.

12. Unless you know exactly what bike you want and the right size for you, head to a good local bike shop. Their advice is invaluable and could save you from an expensive mistake.

13. Second-hand bikes can often stretch your budget to a better model than you could afford to buy new. Just make sure you are buying from its genuine owner.

14. Wherever you buy your bike from, insist on a test ride; this can help you decide if it is really the right bike for you.

15. Shops often organise demo days where you can try multiple bikes from different brands. When heading to a demo day, try to keep as many things the same as when you normally ride, so you can home in on the details of the bike you are testing. Wear your own favourite riding kit and bring your own shoes and pedals if you use them.

16. Take some measurements from your current bike (if it's one you are happy with) and ask the dealer for help setting up your demo bike, so it fits you properly.

17. If you are test riding a full-suspension bike, make sure that the set-up has been adjusted for your weight and riding style, as this will make a huge difference to how the bike feels.

18. Don't base your decision on something that can easily be changed, such as the stem length or the saddle.

19. You can swap your bike saddle for one that is wider, narrower, softer or harder to suit your personal preference.

20. Buying a bike needs careful weighing up of the options and objective testing to make sure you are making the right choice, but don't forget a bike should be fun! Your new bike should put a grin on your face and make you excited to ride. You'll know it's the right bike when you don't want to get off it!

21. Buy the bike.

22. Don't wait until you perceive yourself to be fit enough or fast enough to buy the bike you want. There are no qualifications to getting a good bike. Buy it, ride it, enjoy it.

23. You never regret the bike you bought, only the bike you didn't.

GETTING PEDALLING (24–40)

24. Before you leave with your new purchase, make sure you know how the brakes and gears work. Obvious, right? But you wouldn't be the first person to be flummoxed by the twisty/flicky/tappy shifters on their new machine.

25. Before you ride your bike for the first time, make sure you know which is the front brake and which is the rear brake.

26. When you want to stop, squeeze your brakes on slowly and progressively. Watch out for your front brake, it's super powerful. If you grab your front brake sharply, it can stop the bike very suddenly.

27. Here's a really quick way to get a ballpark saddle height. With your bottom on the saddle and your hands on the handlebars in your normal riding position, place your heel on the pedal. The pedal needs to be at six o'clock, directly at the bottom of the pedal stroke. With your leg fully extended you should be sat square in the saddle, not leaning to the side, and your heel should be in firm contact with the pedal, not hovering above it. When the pedal is then placed in the correct position under the ball of your foot, it will allow for the correct bend in your knee.

28. If it's been a while since you last cycled, have a play around on your bike before you head out on to the road or trail. To cycle safely you need to be confident riding with only one hand on the handlebars (for signalling) and be able to brake safely and quickly.

29. If you haven't ridden for ages, it will come back quickly. You never forget. It is just like riding a bike!

30. Cadence is the speed you pedal, the number of pedal revolutions per minute (rpm). Fast pedalling (90–100rpm) is the speed most experienced road cyclists aim for, but 60rpm, one full pedal stroke per second, is about normal when you first start cycling.

31. Make sure you aren't lazy about gear changing; shift as often as you need to maintain the same cadence throughout your ride (except when sprinting or on steep climbs).

32. When riding off-road, your cadence will be slightly lower and more variable, so you can handle the challenges of the terrain.

The author with 'Cyclista Emily' – women's cycling kit designer – in Mallorca.   © *John Walsh*

BASICS (1-161)

33. While there has been a lot of research into different pedalling cadences, one of the most interesting studies found that when the subjects were allowed to pedal the way they wanted to, instead of trying a cadence faster or slower than their preferred rate, they performed best. So, pedal the way you want to, and it will probably be right for you.*

34. Flats or clipped-in? It's really your choice. Some styles of riding favour flats, but for most road, gravel or trail riding, clipless pedals are of benefit.

35. One of the first things to clear up about clipless pedals is why they are called clipless when you 'clip-in' to them. Bike pedals originally had toe clips and straps, but in 1984 a ski-bindings company called Look decided to apply the same technology to bike shoes, allowing cyclists to use a cleat on the sole of their shoes to 'clip-in' to the mechanism in their pedals. Toe clips and straps were made redundant, so the 'clipless' pedal was born.

36. Being clipped into your pedals will help you feel more at one with the bike. Your feet are less likely to slip off as you pedal or shift your weight around. You can also pedal more fluidly as your pedals and cranks become an extension of your body.

37. You might worry about what will happen if you can't get your feet out in time when you stop or if you crash. Compared with the old-style toe clips, clipless pedals are safer. To release your shoe, it just requires a firm twist of your foot. If you were to crash, the pedals automatically release, making it much less likely that you will remain attached to your bike.

38. To avoid the classic sideways crash, remember to unclip your feet *before* you come to a stop.

39. If you are mountain biking and haven't fully mastered the skill of bunny-hopping, being clipped in allows you to cheat a little bit in getting your wheels off the ground.

40. Don't pedal through puddles on the road – you never know how deep they are or if they are concealing any hazards. Do pedal through puddles off-road, because riding around them leads to braiding or widening of the trail, which can lead to trail erosion and environmental damage.

KIT AND CLOTHING (41–58)

41. Temperature regulation is all about layering and having a range of versatile clothes that you can add or remove easily, depending on the weather.

42. In winter, maintaining a comfortable temperature throughout your ride begins with insulating and protecting your chest and torso. Your core houses your vital organs – your body depends on keeping it a stable temperature. If your core gets cold, your body's defence mechanism is to stop sending warm blood out to your limbs and reserve it for your vital organs. To keep your arms, legs, feet and hands feeling warm, you need to keep your core warm.

43. When it comes to keeping warm, it is wind chill more than getting wet that you need to watch out for. Whether your skin is damp from sweat or rain, add a cold wind and you are at risk of feeling your temperature plummet.

---

* https://journals.lww.com/acsm-msse/Fulltext/2007/06000/Effect_of_Pedaling_Technique_on_Mechanical.14.aspx

Crossing the Miller's Dale Viaduct, Monsal Trail, Derbyshire, England. © *Dave Parry*

44. When reading the weather forecast before a ride, don't forget to check wind strength and direction. Some forecasts will give you a 'feels like' indicator which combines air temperature and wind strength.

45. When choosing your outfit, there are three factors to consider: the weather, the ride you are doing and the terrain. On slower rides and commutes, where you might be waiting at traffic lights and so on, you need to dress a little warmer. On road rides with your mates, thrashing each other up every hill, you might be able to skip the mid layer, but as soon as you stop you will cool down rapidly.

46. If you are mountain biking, you can get very warm climbing or pushing uphill, but feel a chill if you are waiting at the top or descending, so a spare mid layer in your pack is really handy.

47. In winter your knees need covering. That's a non-negotiable fact. Your knee joints need to be protected from the cold if you don't want to have creaking joints and painful ligaments.

48. The chamois or pad in your shorts can make a real difference to your comfort while cycling, but it needs to work for your body shape. Pads come in many different styles and it's the cut, fit and position in the shorts that makes the difference, not just the depth of the padding.

49. When trying on new shorts, adopt a riding position so you can feel how the bib and leg gripper will sit. Yes, you will feel like a wally, but it's the only way to know how they fit on the bike.

50. Don't opt for doubling up on your shorts. They are designed to be worn next to skin; the extra movement and seams in multiple layers cause more problems than they solve. Shorts need washing after every ride with an antibacterial detergent that works at 30 °C to prevent damage to the Lycra®. Halo ProActive Sports Wash is a great option – it works at a low temperature and is antifungal and antibacterial.

51. Carrying a spare extra layer can transform your day if you encounter a sudden rain shower or a cold wind. If you forget your spare layer, a newspaper shoved down the front of your jersey works just as well. A bin bag makes a great windproof and showerproof garment in an emergency.

52. Technical cycling kit can be pricey, but is well worth the investment if it makes rides more enjoyable and more frequent because you aren't avoiding bad weather.

BASICS (1-161)

53. Very-well-turned-out cyclist Rick Stuart suggests, 'If you're fretting over spending £250 on a pair of bike shoes, check out the prices in some designer stores for "fashion sneakers" first, and you'll easily be convinced your spending is but a piffle.'

54. If you are still worried about the cost of kit, then ride your bike more as it will reduce the 'cost per wear', making each purchase better value.

55. When racing in the rain, unless very cold, you are better off with bare skin rather than arm or leg warmers that will get increasingly wet and soggy.

56. It's a bit old-school now, but when racing in cold and wet weather use embrocation. It gives the sensation of warmth by encouraging blood flow to the skin.

57. Covering your legs with Vaseline® or baby oil helps the rain to bead and roll off. Simon Warren of *100 Climbs* insists this is a good idea!

58. GORE-TEX SHAKEDRY™ is the material used in the current 'ultimate' waterproofs for cycling – it breathes, it stretches and water just beads and shakes off. Look for it in premium jackets. Castelli's Gabba has become a firm rider favourite – it feels like a jersey but protects like a jacket.

BIKE KIT (59-66)

59. Helmets are not required by law in the UK. Whether you wear a helmet or not is a personal choice. I've got so used to wearing a helmet that it feels odd to not wear one.

60. Different types of cycling have different designs of helmet to cope with the demands of the sport so, as with choosing a bike, think about the type of riding you want to do before buying.

61. Gloves aren't just about keeping your hands warm. Off-road, or when intentionally going fast on a road, bike gloves are safety kit. Gravel rash to the palms is really unpleasant.

62. Sunglasses aren't just for keeping the sun out of your eyes and posing, they are also safety kit. Grit or bugs in your eyes can cause real damage; if your eyes water it can impair your vision; if you wear contact lenses, your eyes can dry out.

63. You can get clear glasses for night-time riding, yellow-tinted glasses for low visibility and glasses with changeable lenses. Another option is photochromic lenses, which react to the amount of light and change as needed. This is my preferred choice as you don't have to have more than one pair!

64. Proper bike bottles are the best way of carrying fluids on your bike. The plastic bottles that water, pop or juice come in are too thin and oddly shaped to work in a bottle cage. They burst, bounce out or explode in your face when you try to drink. A bike bottle costs just a few quid and lasts for ages. I think they also breed in secret, as I can't open a kitchen cupboard without one falling out.

65. Bike bottles need to be kept scrupulously clean to avoid tasting weird or growing mould. If a quick whizz through the dishwasher isn't enough then use a sterilising tablet. The type you get for cleaning false teeth works wonders.

66. Tubes, tubulars or tubeless? There are a lot of ways to keep your wheels running on a cushion of air. They all work. For some reason, riders get particularly passionate about which is best. It's a horses for courses situation; like choosing the right bike, a lot depends on what you are using them for.

SITTING COMFORTABLY (67–81)

67. Don't ignore your body – riding a bike should not hurt! If you are feeling pain anywhere, it is your body telling you something is wrong. With the right advice, there will be a solution.

68. How comfortable you are when sitting on your bike is about more than just your saddle. Saddle height and reach to the handlebars influences your pelvic angle and weight distribution. If you have any aches, pains or saddle sores, start with getting your bike properly fitted to you by a bike-fit expert.

69. In the words of bike-fit guru and physiotherapist Phil Burt, 'Your bike is adjustable, and your body is adaptable.' You can adjust your bike to fit your physiology, but you can also work on your own soft-tissue strength and flexibility to improve your posture on your bike.

70. If you feel discomfort at the front of your pelvis, lower back or in your wrists, the reach of your bike (how much you lean forward) towards the handlebars may be wrong.

71. Discomfort in your ankle or knee joints suggests your saddle height may be wrong for you.

72. Posture is everything and you need good core strength to maintain your riding position. Think of your bike saddle as a bar stool you perch on, not an armchair that you slump in.

73. I once got a phone call at work from a gentleman who was concerned as his penis had gone numb after a long ride. Saddle sores and intimate numbness can ruin cycling – don't be afraid or embarrassed to get help. However, I'm not sure my advice of 'leaving it alone for a while' was the best help I could have offered.

74. Pressure on the pudendal nerve, which runs through the middle of the base of the penis and perineum, can lead to numbness and erectile dysfunction. There are solutions. This was the reason the gap saddle was first invented.

75. Gap saddles can work for some women, but not all; it really depends on your own shape and tissues. For some, the sensitive areas fit within the gap; for others, their tissue folds overlap the gaps, actually increasing the pressure rather than helping.

76. Finding the right saddle – whatever your comfort issue – is down to trial and error. You need a saddle that fits with your own unique soft tissue presentation.

77. There are some general rules of thumb for saddle choice: your saddle offers the best support when its width correlates with the width of your sitting bones.

78. You can measure the distance between your sitting bones by sitting on a bit of memory foam and measuring between (from centre to centre) the two dents left by the pointy bits of your bum. Some bike shops offer this as part of saddle purchasing.

79. Once you find a saddle that works for you, buy two or experience genuine heartbreak when that style is discontinued.

80. Overriding every one of these other factors is position. You can buy the best saddle, wear the best shorts and slap on the chamois cream, but if your position is wrong, it is compromising every part of you.

81. Check your saddle as part of your regular bike maintenance, or after a crash, as it is easy to knock your saddle out of alignment. A saddle that is a few degrees off-centre can leave you sitting twisted in the saddle; a knock to the front or rear of the saddle can move it slightly nose-up or nose-down.

BASICS (1-161)

ROAD CRAFT (82-114)

82. When you watch a professional cyclist, they have a beautifully smooth, fast technique. In cycling terms, this is sometimes referred to as *souplesse*. A great cyclist makes pedalling look effortless, even when they are trying really hard.

83. In the early 2000s very high cadences became fashionable, partly thanks to Lance Armstrong, who favoured incredibly fast leg speeds. Like many things the pros do, you don't necessarily have to emulate it.

84. While riders are often told that high cadences are better and more efficient, the 'optimal' cadence is still a subject for debate and academic research, with no definitive answer. However, if you are slowly chugging the pedals around at 50–60rpm then you will benefit from practising an increased cadence – it will do your knees a favour, if nothing else!

85. You can increase the speed and *souplesse* of your pedalling by doing a few bike drills. If you include these as part of a warm-up or rest day ride, then it takes no extra time or effort to work on your pedalling technique.

86. Practise spin-ups, where you start in a light gear and then pedal as fast as you can and hold it for 30 seconds. This will gradually increase your maximum cadence and develop your ability to do this without bouncing around on the saddle. It's good to make this a regular part of your warm-up on every ride.

87. The single biggest thing a cyclist has to overcome to go faster is wind resistance. Pushing your bike and body through the air accounts for your greatest energy expenditure, and the faster you go the more resistance you encounter.

88. Don't be a sail. Reduce your frontal area by tucking in your elbows, bringing your chest lower to the bars and riding in the drops, if you're on a road bike.

89. Embrace the figure-hugging power of Lycra. Make sure the clothing you wear is tight fitting and doesn't inflate in the wind. When you want to go fast, zip up your jacket or jersey.

90. Braking robs you of momentum and you have to pedal harder to accelerate back up to speed, which is tiring.

91. Riders over-brake in a variety of situations, but it is nearly always down to lack of confidence. Confidence can be gained with practice.

92. Cornering is where effective braking will make the most difference to your average speed, so practise your technique.

93. Brake only in a straight line; use your front brake sparingly as it is the most powerful. Squeeze and release rather than dragging your brakes.

94. When you ride with others, you all share responsibility for the safety of everyone in the group. From pointing out potholes to checking junctions — it's important to remember your actions will influence those around you.

95. When riding in a group, the best road formation is side-by-side with the pair behind following in a line. *(Figure 1)*

96. Cyclists are allowed to ride in pairs under the UK Highway Code (Rule 66). Small, compact groups make it easier for cars to pass than long, strung-out lines. *(Figure 2)*

97. Be traffic aware and single out (ride in single file) where needed and stick to small groups of six (with gaps between) so cars don't get stuck behind you. This is just courteous to other road users.

98. Never 'half-wheel', unless you want to fall out with the rest of the group. Half-wheeling, where a rider always rides half a wheel ahead of the rider next to them, encourages the other rider to go harder to bring their wheel level with yours, gradually upping the pace and putting the pressure on everyone behind as well.

99. Protect your front wheel. If you are following behind someone else don't overlap their rear wheel – if they suddenly swerve or move out around an obstacle, they will take your front wheel out from under you.

100. Don't watch the wheel in front; keep your head up and watch what is going on around you. With practice, you will be able to hold your distance simply by knowing how far away the rider's bottom in your peripheral vision should be.

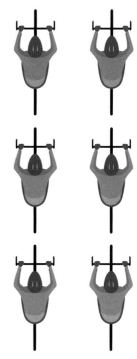

FIGURE 1

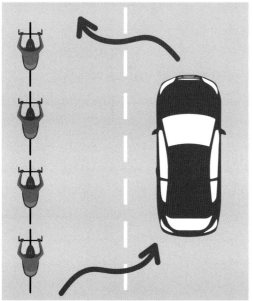

FIGURE 2

11

stop

slowing

left turn

right turn

pothole

debris

approaching a hazard

train tracks

pull through

wave

FIGURE 3

BASICS (1-161)

101. Use hand signals to point out hazards and movements in the group. Raise your hand above your head to indicate *stop*. When your speed is *slowing*, extend your arm with palm down and move your hand up and down. Extend the appropriate arm away from your body to indicate a *left turn* and a *right turn*. To warn the group about a *pothole*, extend your arm to the side and point at it; the signal for *debris* is similar – extend your arm to the side and wave your hand from side to side. If you're *approaching a hazard*, use the arm on the same side as the hazard, place it behind your back and point – this shows riders which way to go to avoid it. When you're approaching *train tracks*, point at the tracks and move your finger back and forth horizontally. When riding in the 'through and off' formation (*tip 107*) and you're at the front and want to *pull through* to the back, flick your elbow. If someone lets you through at a junction, *wave* to say thanks. *(Figure 3)*

102. Hand signals are universal and can be used when you no longer have the available breath to talk or if you're in a group of riders of mixed nationalities.

103. Shouting out every pothole can be like the boy who cries wolf – people start to tune it out. Constant shouting can make a group feel nervous and jumpy.

104. If you have riders close behind you, ride smoothly and maintain an even speed, pointing out obstacles that they won't be able to see.

105. If you need to get out of the saddle, don't stand up and stop pedalling – your sudden change in speed will make it hard for the rider behind to avoid your wheel. Keep your momentum by pedalling as you rise up out of the saddle, in an action a bit like climbing up stairs.

106. When riding in the wind as a group, one line will be sheltering the other, so make sure that the weaker riders are benefitting from the protection.

107. To get the most benefit from being in a group, and to allow everyone to have a chance to work and rest, you can organise the bunch to start 'through and off'. Two parallel lines can work together, with the 'working line' protecting the 'resting line' from the wind. *(Figure 4)*

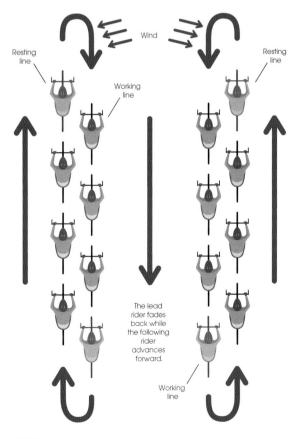

Resting line

Wind

Resting line

Working line

The lead rider fades back while the following rider advances forward.

Working line

FIGURE 4

BASICS (1-161)

108. The length of turns depends on the type of riding and who you are riding with. On a steady group ride where you might be out for hours and everyone is chatting, 20-minute turns are fine. In a race or a break where you want to keep the pace high, changes are just a few seconds. It feels like you never get a rest!

109. It's generally considered a bit rude to never do a turn, unless you are clearly struggling and doing all you can just to stay in the group. If you are strong enough to take your turn, you should.

110. You started together; you finish together – this is the number one rule of 'no-drop' group rides.

111. If you are a stronger rider, you can help a weaker rider stay on the wheel and in the group by gently placing a hand on their lower back. Ask first!

112. If you are a weaker rider and someone gives you a shove or a push, don't feel insulted. It keeps the group together and the pace higher for everyone. As soon as you are out of the 'bubble' of the group and the elastic snaps you will wish that you had done everything you could to hold that wheel, including accepting a push.

113. Male riders – we female riders can tell the difference between an opportunistic grope and actually helping us to stay in the bunch. If I'm chatting to you, I don't need your hand on my bum. If I'm obviously out of breath, then a push might be welcome. Again, ask first!

114. A few clubs still operate a more ruthless approach to group riding. Those who get dropped from the back are left to finish alone. It's easy to knock this approach as selfish, but I credit the fear of being abandoned and getting lost for teaching me how to ride fast and cling on to a wheel!

TRAIL CRAFT (115–131)

115. Heels down. This is the golden rule for everything off-road. You can't ride powerfully and dynamically if you are pointing your toes like a ballet dancer in *Swan Lake*. Pushing down through your heels improves your bike's traction and your weight distribution.

116. Heels down; pedals level; bottom hovering just above the saddle; elbows bent; knees bent; head up; big grin. This is the 'attack' position, which is the foundation of every technique off-road. *(Figure 5)*

117. The big grin is essential. It helps keep your whole body relaxed.

118. With your elbows and knees bent and your bottom off the saddle, your weight is positioned centrally over the bike so there is space for the bike to move around underneath you. Relaxing and bending your knees and arms allows them to flex like shock absorbers. You are moving with the bumps of the trail, not fighting against it.

119. Look at where you want to go, not at what scares you. One hundred per cent of the time: if you stare at the unnerving drop or frightening tree stump, that is where your front wheel will end up.

FIGURE 5 © *John Coefield*

120. Momentum is your friend. It might feel daunting, but a little bit of speed will help your bike roll over the top of obstacles rather than bump and jar against everything, throwing you off-line.

121. Lack of commitment when tackling an obstacle is frequently the reason for failure. If you approach something tentatively, without enough speed or with your feet not firmly on the pedals, there is a good chance it will go wrong.

122. Commit, commit, commit.

123. For steep inclines, pull yourself forward on the handlebars, keep some weight on the front wheel to stop it lifting up and keep some weight over your rear wheel to maintain traction and drive.

124. For steep descents, it's more about keeping your weight towards the back of the bike to counteract the pull of gravity.

125. Always cover your brake levers – disc brakes are so powerful you can easily pull them on with one finger, so get into the habit of riding with your index finger covering them.

126. Learn which is your front and which is your back brake. Stopping your front wheel sharply will either result in a front wheel skid and loss of control or a quick exit over the handlebars.

127. Modulation is a word often used to describe mountain bike braking – it refers to the range of braking power available to a rider. Squeeze your brakes on gently and progressively, don't just grab a handful!

128. Keep your head up and look far enough ahead down the trail to allow time to brake early. Brake early, before you need to turn or tackle a trail obstacle, then let your bike roll.

129. If you lock your wheels, you have no grip or traction, so avoid jamming on the brakes. But with skill (and a lot of practice) you can use a controlled skid or front wheel 'stoppie' to change direction.

130. Tyre and suspension pressures make a massive difference to how your bike feels to ride and its grip. Check pressures before every ride and one day you might find yourself instinctively adjusting pressures to suit different terrain.

131. Crashing is part and parcel of extending your skills off-road and if you never crash you probably aren't pushing your limits as far as you are capable of, whether that is through choice, fear or lack of confidence. However, crashing is not an essential part of having fun off-road! Enjoy riding within your skill level and comfort zone.

SEASONAL CYCLING (132–149)

132. Cycling isn't a seasonal sport. You can ride all year round, provided that you have the right kit and the right attitude.

133. One of the strongest reasons for cycling through winter is maintaining the fitness you acquired during summer. There is nothing more demoralising than getting on your bike in the spring and struggling up a climb you found easy just a few months before.

134. With short winter days it's even more important to get outside in the light when you can. Spending time in natural light is an important part of keeping your body in sync with the seasons. It aids vitamin D production and can help with mental health issues, such as seasonal affective disorder.

BASICS (1-161)

135. When it comes to winter cycling, don't be a hero – some days are just too icy or too windy to be outside safely. Have a day off; use the rollers; go on Zwift. Don't miss eight weeks of riding with a broken leg.

136. Rain is a different story. No one ever shrunk in the rain. If you won't ride in the rain, you won't do much outside riding in the UK, ever. If you don't train in the rain, you won't have the skills necessary to race safely in wet weather.

137. Mudguards keep your bottom dry and keep muddy spray off your bike, which will help it stay clean. It also helps stop a fountain of muddy water spraying directly into the eyes of the person behind you.

138. If you want to ride fast on a mountain bike in wet, muddy weather, a front mudguard is almost indispensable. Without one, you ride directly into the flung-up mud and water from your front wheel which will obscure your vision and be very unpleasant.

139. Previously dry roads can become treacherous in the first few minutes of rain, as oil and dust create a really slippery surface. Once enough rain has fallen to wash it into the gutter, conditions improve again. Take care, especially if you can see the telltale oily rainbow.

140. Avoid riding on and especially cornering on white lines, drain covers or tram tracks when it is wet. If you need to cross a slip hazard (this includes cattle grids in the dry) always approach them square on, never at an angle.

141. Get yourself a really good set of lights and you can ride day or night all year round.

142. Night-time riding can make an easy, familiar trail feel fun and exciting again.

143. For off-road riding use two lights. A bar-mounted light provides a flood of light in front of you and a helmet light illuminates where you are looking as you turn your head. This is essential if you are riding on twisty singletrack and you will want to see round the next corner.

144. On roads, remember to light up your bike from the side, not just the front and rear, so you are visible while riding across junctions.

145. Put reflectors and lights on the parts of your bike that move, such as pedals and wheels, as moving lights attract the eye more.

146. Wear reflective clothing or lights on your body; not only will it help you be seen while riding but it helps to make you visible if for any reason you are not on your bike.

147. Cyclists love a sharp tan line. It's another one of those subtle ways of boasting about how many hours you have spent on your bike in the sun. To achieve the look, you need to make sure all your shorts, jerseys and socks are exactly the same length every time you get on your bike.

148. But, with the length of time you spend outside on your bike, never skimp on sunscreen. I know several cyclists who have had skin cancers removed, so this tip is personal.

149. Put your water bottles in the freezer overnight and you will have a constant supply of cold water throughout your ride as your drink defrosts.

CLIMBING HILLS (150–161)

150. Hills are an inevitable part of cycling. At some point you are going to have to get over them. Whether you want to master climbing mountains, or just stop fearing the hill on the route to work, you need to work on your head as well as your legs.

151. On-road or off-road, as you approach the hill carry as much speed as you can into the start of it, particularly if you are approaching it from a downhill.

152. Look ahead, as you will need to change down into an easier gear before the hill becomes steep, as shifting under load puts a lot of strain on your chain.

153. If you attack the bottom of a climb too fast, your lungs might burn and your legs 'pop' before you reach the top. Look ahead and, if you can see the top, try to pace your effort.

154. It is better to start the climb at a comfortable, manageable pace, maybe even a little bit easier than you think you are capable of, and only accelerate once the top comes into sight.

155. Keep your momentum over the top of the climb instead of easing off as soon as you reach the top. Change into a bigger gear and continue to pedal into the start of the descent to keep your speed up until gravity takes over.

156. Climbing technical terrain on a mountain bike is about skill as well as the grunt factor of how much power you have. Keep your head up and scan the trail so you can make good line choices and avoid the big roots, bumps and rocks that can jar your front wheel and make you lose your momentum.

157. We have all had the experience of searching for an easier gear, only to find out we are already in the lowest gear we have. In this situation you have nothing left to do but grind it out.

158. Alternating between sitting and standing while climbing can help as you can use your body weight, not just your leg power, to push down on the pedals.

159. When a hill gets really steep and you have no more gears left, zigzag across the slope to take the sting out of the gradient.

160. If you do need to stop and put a foot down it can be very hard to get going again. Angle your bike across or slightly down the slope as you set off again. Turn in a wide arc to give you time to get both feet settled on the pedals before you turn your bike uphill again.

161. Did you know that you can change the gear ratios on your bike to make climbing easier? If you are always running out of gears, ask your local bike mechanic for some advice.

You can't beat the service you get from a good bike shop, especially when they've got your all-new ebike. © *John Coefield*

Always pick the right tool for the job.   © John Coefield

002

MAINTENANCE (162–313)

'What can't be fixed with cable ties and duct tape?'

MAINTENANCE (162–313)

PRE-RIDE CHECKS (162–177)

162. Checking your bike before every ride is a quick and easy job to do and could prevent serious injury.

163. With practice, a thorough bike check doesn't take long and will quickly become part of your normal pre-ride routine, like finding your helmet or gulping down a coffee!

164. An M-check is used by many mechanics, coaches and bike riders as a way of remembering what parts of the bike to check and in what order. Doing it the same way every time makes it less likely that you'll miss something. *(Figure 6)*

165. Start at the front wheel and work to the back wheel. Check that the quick release which holds your front wheel in place is tightly closed and check that when you move the wheel from side to side it doesn't wobble.

166. Pick the front of your bike up and spin the wheel – check the tyres have no worn areas or cuts in them. Check the wheel spins smoothly and isn't buckled or rubbing on the brakes. Pinch the tyres and check they are inflated to the correct pressure.

167. Put the wheel down again and move up to the handlebars. When you rock the bike backwards and forwards, can you feel any knocking or movement in the headset (where the handlebars attach to the frame)?

168. Swing the handlebars from side to side to see if they move freely.

169. Use the front brake to stop the wheel. Does it stop quickly and firmly?

170. Look over the long diagonal down tube of the bike to the bottom bracket where the pedals attach. Check there are no big bumps or scrapes. Grab both crank arms and pedals, give them a good tug and check your pedals spin round freely where they join the crank.

171. Wobble your bottle cage to check it isn't loose and check the bottle isn't going to fall out.

172. Follow up from the bottom bracket to your saddle, check your seat post clamp is tight so the saddle won't suddenly drop down or twist.

173. Grab your saddle and try to nudge it up and down or forward and back to see if it is secure where it is clamped to the bike.

174. Follow the tubes behind your saddle down to the rear wheel, checking for any damage.

175. At the rear wheel check the wheel is securely locked in the frame and repeat the checks on the wheel that you did at the front – picking up the bike to spin the wheel and checking the tyre. Test that your back brake is powerful, stops the wheel with control and isn't rubbing.

176. If you do nothing else do this. Lift your bike around five centimetres off the ground, then drop it down. You are listening for any rattles, clunks, thuds or noises you don't normally hear – and at worst something dropping off! A beautifully maintained bike will be almost silent.

177. The M-check is designed to spot problems, but it doesn't go deeply into how well your gears shift, whether cables are worn or if bearings need changing. For that you need a full service.

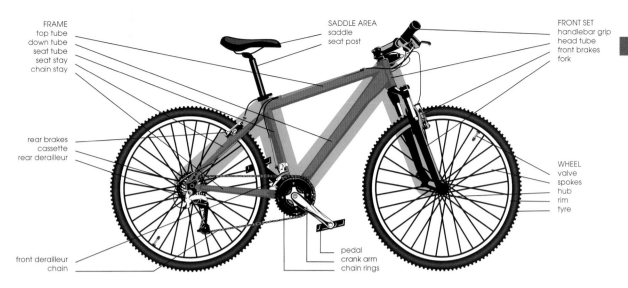

FIGURE 6 The M-check (*tips 164–175*) and parts of a bike. © *Shutterstock/Iurii Kalmatsui*

THINGS TO CARRY (178–200)

178. Regardless of the bike you are riding or how far you are going, always take the basics with you every time you leave the house.

179. Make sure you have the right size of *inner tube* for the type of bike you are riding. Nothing is more frustrating than pulling out your tube to discover it's a 26-inch when you need a 29-inch for your mountain bike tyre.

180. Yes, you will get kudos from your ride mates if you can whip off a tyre without levers, but if your hands are cold or wet or the tyre is tight then *tyre levers* can help you to get the tyre off faster. No one will be impressed if they are kept shivering while you struggle.

181. Give your *pump* a check every now and again if you haven't used it for a bit.

182. Snapping a chain on a ride can mean game over if you can't fix it. A *chain tool* and/or *quick link* means a five-minute repair job instead of a long walk home.

183. A *multi-tool* is a lightweight, easy way to make sure you have everything you need. With a decent multi-tool, you can pretty much strip and rebuild your entire bike!

184. Always carry enough *money* for a coffee, some food and a phone call.

185. You can take off the front plate of your stem or pull out your seat pin and stuff a fiver inside as an emergency stash.

186. It's unlikely that anyone would be going out on their bike without a *phone* but, aside from getting photos for Instagram, your phone could be really helpful in case of an incident.

187. The further you go from help, or if you are off-road, the more self-sufficient you need to be and the more items you need to carry.

188. If you're out mountain biking, carry a set of spare *brake pads*; in poor conditions you could easily go through a set in a day ride.

189. A *gear cable* is relatively light and easy to carry, so you might as well pop one in your bag. A snapped cable can be easily fixed with a spare.

190. If you are heading out into remote areas, where it could take time to be rescued, it's good to carry some form of *shelter* (such as a survival bag, bivvy bag or tarp) to keep you warm and dry if someone is injured.

191. Carry a *shock pump*, as you may want to adjust suspension pressure to suit the conditions.

192. Wet and mucky or even dry and dusty conditions can leave your chain creaking or grinding. A rag and a little bit of *lube* can help sort it out mid ride.

193. A snapped *mech hanger* can ruin your day and leave you having to single-speed your bike to get back home. Carrying a spare that fits your bike will make it a quick job to replace, so your ride can go on.

194. The further you are from getting help quickly the more advanced the *first aid kit* you carry should be. A minimum is gloves (for the first aider), a way of cleaning a wound and something to cover it up with.

195. An assortment of old *bolts* can get you out of sticky situations. A chain ring bolt, cleat bolt and a couple of M4 and M5 bolts will help you put your bike back together.

196. What can't be fixed with *cable ties* and *duct tape*?

197. A single *spoke* with a nipple attached can help sort out a snapped spoke. Again, they are light so you might as well carry one as it could get you out of a fix.

198. If you run out of inner tubes a *patch repair kit* can be invaluable and the only way to get inflated again.

199. Plastic zip-lock sandwich bags are brilliant for keeping your phone or bank cards dry in your back pocket or trail bag.

200. Sandwich bags are also great for carrying your own *trail mix*. A few nuts, some jelly babies and dried fruit shoved in a bag for a lucky dip every time you feel peckish.

FIXING PUNCTURES (201–219)

201. Punctures are as inevitable a part of cycling as hills and headwinds. While they are invariably annoying, they don't have to ruin your ride. With a bit of practice and the right tools, they can be fixed in five minutes.

202. Always carry the spares you need with you. Even if you aren't confident fixing your own puncture (yet), you may be lucky enough to find someone to help you, provided that you have the right stuff.

203. When you remove your wheel, lean your bike up somewhere or lay it down on the grass, drive side up. Don't ever put your bike upside down resting on the bars and saddle – it scratches and damages your levers and any GPS or bike computer on your bars (and it gives a certain type of old-school roadie the cold shivers).

204. Completely deflate your tyre by depressing the valve to let all remaining air out. With the wheel on the floor or resting on your shoes, start with the valve and both hands at twelve o'clock. Using both hands working away from each other, squeeze and pull any slack in the tyre down to the six o'clock position. You should now be able to gently roll the tyre off the rim; if it is still tight, use a tyre lever to hook under the bead and release it from one side.

Puncture repair lessons with Cycling UK. © *Patrick Trainor*

205. Check your tyre; you need to find the culprit otherwise you will just puncture your new tube. Do a visual inspection first for any thorns, stones or cuts. Next, run your fingers gently around the inside of the tyre being careful and slow, just in case there is anything sharp. If you can't find anything, check where the hole in the inner tube is for a clue. If there are two small holes close together it could have been a pinch puncture, so you're less likely to have anything sharp in your tyre.

206. Even if you find something keep going and check again – there might be more than one thorn that has found its way in.

207. Seat the tyre back on the rim, making sure the bead is hooked under. If you want to be super-pro, now is the time to line up your logos on your tyre with the logos on your wheel. Unwrap your inner tube and hang it round your neck or give it to someone to hold. Be careful not to let it touch the ground. Inflate the inner tube slightly until it holds its shape. Put the valve through the valve hole and tuck the inner tube inside the tyre.

208. Put the valve at twelve o'clock, make sure it is hanging straight down, and then, with both hands working away from each other, push the tyre back over the rim, so the bead sits under the hook of the rim, taking care not to pinch the inner tube. When you get to six o'clock the tyre may start to feel tight.

209. You can now pick the wheel up and brace it against your hips to try and push the final part of the tyre over. (This bracing part is a very good reason for avoiding white or pale coloured shorts – in case you needed one.) If it still won't go on, start again at the top and push/pull the tyre until you have worked as much slack as possible down to the bottom, and try again.

210. Use your tyre levers as a last resort as it makes it more likely to pinch the inner tube. Use the lever to hook and lift the tyre over the rim so the bead sits under the hook of the rim.

211. Once the tyre is on, check all the way round that you can't see any inner tube sticking out and that the bead is correctly seated. Give the valve a little wiggle up and down to make sure it is properly in place, then start to inflate your tyre.

212. Once the tyre is up to the correct pressure, give it a spin and check again for any lumps or bulges. If it all looks good put the wheel back on your bike, checking of course that it is securely locked in, and the brakes are correctly positioned and working again.

213. If someone in your group gets a puncture check your own tyres too. There is nothing more annoying than someone else in the group discovering a puncture just as you get moving again.

214. If you slit your tyre, then you will need to cover it up otherwise the inner tube will push through and puncture again. A slice of toothpaste tube, a section of old tyre or even an empty energy gel wrapper can be placed inside the tube to keep the inner tube in place.

215. If you have fancy, deep-section wheels carry a valve extender. A valve extender can adapt any length of inner tube valve to fit your wheel. Useful if you run out of your own tubes!

216. If you can't get a road tyre up to full pressure, cut the top off the valve cap and screw it on upside down to use a garage forecourt compressor pump.

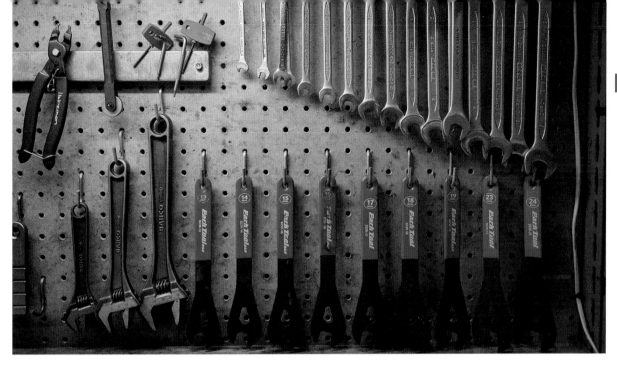

Make sure you've got the right tool for the job. © *John Coefield*

217. If you don't have a spare tube or puncture repair kit, you are best off phoning for a taxi or begging a passing cyclist. Yes, someone will tell you about the time they stuffed their tyre with grass or attached the tyre to the rim with cable ties but, in reality, it's a pain that will barely get you home, although you can at least say you tried.

218. When choosing tyres, look for those with an anti-puncture band or Kevlar strip. You will pay a little bit more but if you ride a lot of miles, it is worth it. Nothing will completely protect you from punctures, but it will reduce them to only a rare annoyance.

219. Tubeless wheels are brilliant when you are using them, but a pain to set up. Tyres have to be seated in such a way that they are air-tight and then latex fluid poured into the tyre. If you get a small puncture the latex fills the hole and seals it when it comes into contact with the air. It's the closest cycling has come (so far) to a solution to punctures.

TRAIL AND ROADSIDE REPAIRS
(220–238)

220. Provided you're looking after your chain, by regularly cleaning and lubricating it, and not using a worn chain, your chain should not snap. In the unlikely event of a snapped chain, it is quick and easy to repair if you have the right tools with you.

221. If you can't fix your chain, you are pretty much scuppered. Unless you are at the top of the hill and your house is at the bottom. Or you are riding with someone mug enough to push you home.

222. If a chain does snap it invariably happens under a heavy load when you are sprinting or climbing a steep hill. The natural consequence of suddenly losing the resistance of the chain is either a heavy knee-to-headset interface or worse a crash. Keep an eye on your chain wear!

223. Most multi-tools have a chain splitter, but they are seldom that good and they can be quite tricky to use. Instead carry a separate chain tool – they are a bit bigger and heavier to carry but the one time you need it will justify the reason for carrying it on all your rides.

Sometimes, the wrong tool is the right tool for the job. © *John Coefield*

224. As chain tools are quite heavy, when weight is an issue, carry a quick link. Rather than trying to rejoin a chain, a quick link allows you to join the two ends together easily without tools.

225. If you haven't got a spare pair of hands to help, you can bend a paper clip to hold the two broken ends close together while you line up the quick link. Keep one in your pack or saddle bag.

226. Make sure you have the correct size for your chain – 7/8-speed, 9-speed, 10-speed, 11-speed or 12-speed.

227. Use electrical tape to secure a quick link on your bars or under your stem, so it's always there when you need it.

228. To use a quick link, take the two ends of your chain and align the pins and outer plates, then pull tight, so they snap together.

229. You can use your bike to snap a quick link into place. Rotate your chain on the bike until the quick link is at the top. With both wheels on the ground, hold your brakes on so your bike doesn't move, then step down hard on the top pedal so the links pull into place.

230. You can use your bike for storing spares, so you never forget them. Spare spokes can be taped inside your seat post. By taking the front plate off your stem you can stash a couple of banknotes for emergencies.

231. Wrap a few good lengths of duct tape and electrical tape around your bike pump, ready to unwind when you need some.

232. If you have two bottle cages you can use one for a bottle stuffed with spares and a waterproof jacket.

233. Hide your cable ties inside your handlebars by removing a bar end plug.

234. If you have a slit in the side wall of a tyre you need to cover it before putting in a new tube, otherwise it will just push through. You could carry a ready-cut piece of an old tyre or a toothpaste tube with you, but if you don't have these then an energy gel packet or a banknote will do the job!

235. Losing a cleat bolt is really annoying and can make clipping in or out difficult. Keep a spare on your bike or in your pack.

236. If a bolt shears for some reason, you may already have a replacement on your bike. Bottle cage bolts are often the same size as stem, seat post and rack bolts.

237. Invariably, the time you need to fix something will be when you are tired or it's cold, raining or getting dark, so practise repairs in the comfort of your own home until you can do them fast. When I was training for a 24-hour solo mountain bike race, I'd set my alarm for 2.00 a.m. to fix a puncture or repair a chain before going back to sleep. It gave me confidence to know I could do these things when sleep deprived.

238. Squealing disc brakes are incredibly irritating for you and everyone around you. Riding in wet weather or getting contamination on the discs from splashing through an oily puddle makes noise almost inevitable. If your previously silent brakes start squealing do some hard, heavy braking (on the flat and in a straight line), as that will help heat the brakes up and evaporate the water off, resulting in increased braking power and less noise.

EBIKES (239–253)

239. Many riders are initially daunted by the idea of looking after their ebike but, if you ignore the battery and drive unit, the rest of the bike is exactly the same as a conventional bike and needs looking after in a similar way.

240. It's very important to keep on top of maintenance and basics like tyre pressure. On a conventional bike, you quickly notice if you are riding on flat tyres or have a sticking bottom bracket but, on an ebike, the motor compensates. You won't notice a change in speed or effort, but your battery will go flat much more quickly.

241. Ebikes work at their optimum around 80rpm. If you pedal very fast, the bike stops giving you the support of pedal-assist. If you pedal very slowly in a hard gear you get more pedal-assist, so the cycling feels easy, but you are using a lot of support, which will decrease your battery range.

242. The extra torque and power of an ebike motor puts more strain on your bike's drivetrain than a conventional bike receives, so you may need to replace components more often.

243. Brake pads need to be checked frequently. As ebikes are heavier and often faster, brake pads wear out more quickly.

244. If you look after your ebike battery and charge in accordance with the manufacturer's advice, then it should last for more than 1,000 complete charge cycles and still have 50 per cent capacity remaining. In reality, batteries will last as long, if not longer, than the useful life of your bike.

245. Many ebike manufacturers use lithium-ion – Li-ion – batteries (the same type as you get in many mobile phones). They like to be charged, so don't let your bike battery run completely flat – top-up the charge after every ride, even if you have only used one bar of battery power.

246. One of the few things that affects Li-ion battery performance is extremes in temperature. If you normally keep your bike outside in a garage or shed during the winter months, you must move the battery inside if temperatures are likely to drop below 10 °C.

247. Batteries discharge more quickly when cold, so if you are riding your ebike in winter weather you will need to charge your battery more frequently than in warmer weather.

248. Hot weather can also interfere with performance, so try not to leave your bike parked up in the sun during a ride. Find it a cool, shady resting spot while you are in the cafe.

249. Range, how far you can go on one charge, has vastly improved since ebikes first came out; 100 to 150 kilometres is pretty standard now. Range is affected by temperature, terrain, riding style, rider weight and how much power you as the rider put in. The less assistance you use, the further you will go on one charge.

250. Don't forget to turn your bike on before you start pedalling! If you start riding and then switch on the motor, you can trigger a system error as there is pressure going through the pedals that the sensor does not expect.

251. Keeping on top of regular software updates is just as important as looking after the mechanical side of the bike.

252. Check connections are secure and cables are not kinked or frayed, but don't go poking around inside connectors or attempt to disassemble a battery. You won't be able to fix it yourself and you will probably just give yourself a nasty electric shock. For any electrical and battery problems you need to go back to the dealer.

253. Problems with error messages? Blank screens? Turn it off then turn it back on again.

BIKE CLEANING (254–274)

254. A good wash down gives you the chance to spot any areas of wear and tear that may soon need fixing. Keep an eye out for frayed cables, deep scratch marks or scuffs, or any fluid leaks around seals on your suspension (if your bike has any), which could indicate a problem.

255. Keeping your bike clean and lubricated will help increase the longevity of components and save you money in the long run.

256. You can do a really thorough wash in 20 minutes and a pretty good effort in less than 10.

257. Through long experience, I have learned that cleaning your bike is easier while the muck and dirt are still wet, so you need less water and effort to wash them off!

258. Contaminated disc brakes will squeal and may lose some of their braking power, so keep all oils away from them. Some people like to take their disc pads out altogether when cleaning their bike to ensure nothing contacts the pads.

259. Dampen your bike with a bucket and sponge. A jet wash is tempting for speed but, unless you are really careful, you can blow water and muck into the bearings which can cause damage.

260. Spray all over with a bike cleaning spray and allow a few moments for it to get to work.

261. Use a soft-bristled brush to work the muck loose then rinse again with clean water.

262. To clean your disc rotors thoroughly, either use a specific bike cleaner (don't go near them with anything designed for vehicles) or use neat alcohol on a lint-free cloth to scrub them.

263. Any contaminants on the surface will transfer to the pads, so be careful not to touch your disc rotors with oily fingers while cleaning your bike.

264. Don't waste time scrubbing your chain – use a chain cleaner that clamps on and pulls your chain through a series of brushes and a bath of degreaser. It's really easy to get great results this way.

265. When spraying lube or frame polish, put your bike in a bike stand and take your wheels off the bike so nothing goes near disc rotors.

266. To save taking your disc pads out, you can protect them from sprays by pulling a latex glove over the whole calliper (or using a plastic sandwich bag).

267. Once your bike is clean and dry, carefully apply a coating of silicone spray to the frame (avoiding getting any on brake pads) to help stop mud sticking to it so it is easier to clean next time.

268. Ordinary furniture polish can do as good a job as expensive bike-specific frame polish.

Choose your bike lube wisely. © John Coefield

269. You don't have to clean all of your bike after every ride, but do degrease and re-lube your chain frequently.

270. Piling more and more lube on your bike, without getting rid of the old, just attracts dirt. This leaves you with a horrible, greasy, black mess, which becomes a grinding paste that accelerates the wear on your cassette and chain.

271. Choose your bike lube wisely. There are different weights for different conditions (wet and dry) and different types of lubrication, including wax as well as oil. Some are thicker and gloopier than others.

272. Seriously consider buying a biodegradable oil, especially if you ride off-road where bike lube could be washed into puddles or streams.

273. Cleaning an ebike means being sparing on the water and avoiding any kind of pressure washer. Use a bucket of warm water and a sponge or cloth to loosen and wipe away compacted dirt and mud.

274. To dry an ebike you can use a hairdryer on a cool setting to ensure all electrical points are free of water.

HOME WORKSHOP (275–297)

275. If you spot problems with your bike during your ride, either deal with them straight away when you get home or make a note to remind yourself. I've lost count of the number of times I've started a bike ride only to then remember the jumping gears, worn-out tyre or creaking bottom bracket I didn't fix after the last ride. Try and be better than me!

276. Bikes are relatively simple machines; most people can do the majority of maintenance at home, as long as you have the right tools and a bit of knowledge.

277. When you don't have knowledge, there is YouTube. There are some brilliant 'how to' videos done by professional bike mechanics.

278. Proprietary tools are the bane of the home mechanic's life. Investing in a brand-specific bottom bracket tool you may only use once is very expensive, but bodging a bike repair with the wrong tool can be even more costly. Buy the tool or take it to a shop.

279. If you want to stand a chance of doing any work on your bike at home properly, you need some decent tools.

280. Replacing chains and cassettes is a simple job to do at home, but you need a chain whip, a cassette remover and a big adjustable spanner.

281. Using quick links makes fixing or swapping chains really easy, but a quick link tool makes it even easier. It takes the tension out of the chain so you can pop links off easily and snap them back together.

282. Don't even think about trying to fix your bike at home without a proper bike stand. This is one purchase that will change your life. No more bending over a bike leaning against a wall – you can see exactly what you are working on at eye level.

283. Get yourself a proper heavy-duty chain tool to use at home. The chain splitters you get on multi-tools are great in a pinch out on the road or trail but too fiddly to use at home.

284. A chain-wear checking tool is a really simple way of checking the health of your chain. They are cheap and easy to use so even if you aren't a natural home mechanic you can manage this task.

285. By replacing part-worn chains you can extend the life of your cassette, getting one cassette for every two or three chains. If you don't replace your chain, your cassette and chain will wear matching grooves into each other, and both will need replacing as a new chain will 'jump' on the cassette and not run smoothly.

286. A full set of ball-ended Allen keys makes everything easier. Invariably, I am always missing the four-millimetre; it often turns up in the washing machine as I shove tools in my back pockets. Maybe we should add a fancy tool apron to this list?

287. Having some really good snips (cable cutters) means no more frayed cable ends or squashed gear housing. You can also use them to neatly crimp the cable end caps. It is the quality of crimping on a cable end cap which distinguishes the amateur mechanic from the pro.

288. If you have a fancy bike, dripping with lots of carbon parts, then a torque wrench is an essential bit of kit. Most manufacturers put the correct tension in newton-metres (N m) on their products. With a correctly calibrated torque wrench you can be sure you are not over-tightening and running the risk of snapped bolts or fractured carbon.

289. Every home with a bike needs a decent, heavy-weight track pump, as pumping up tyres and checking tyre pressure should be part of your pre-ride ritual.

290. But, if you want to get fancy, then an air compressor is brilliant – not just for pumping up tyres, but seating notoriously difficult tubeless tyres and even dispersing dust or water from all the nooks and crevices on your bike. Go on, treat yourself.

MAINTENANCE (162-313)

291. To complete your home workshop you'll need a tool bench or board to keep things tidy – and make it look professional. Kitting out your workshop is not cheap, but if you enjoy fiddling with bikes it is well worth the investment to do it properly.

292. A workshop is not just about tools; you also need a few different greases. Anti-seize, copper slip, red jelly rubber grease for seals, ceramic grease – it looks like the shelf of a pharmacy, but each grease has a specific purpose, so you need a few.

293. It looks totally out of place when you see it in a workshop, but talcum powder, designed for a baby's bottom, is great for running around the inside of new tyres before fitting. It allows the inner tube to move around smoothly, makes it less likely to pinch when you fit it and reduces friction.

294. And for tubeless tyre users? Washing-up liquid squirted around the bead helps create enough of a seal to get those bad boys inflated without making yourself light-headed from pumping. Or just buy a compressor, or a fancy tubeless pump with an air reservoir.

295. Give your bike a service before riding it for the first time or if it has been unused for a while, and after that once every three to six months if you are riding regularly, even if you haven't spotted a problem.

296. Fix problems when they arise! Problems tend to get more expensive the longer they are ignored.

297. Know your limits. There is a lot most people can do at home and there is absolutely no harm in giving it a go, but if you're struggling then get some help from a professional bike mechanic. A smooth-running bike is not just safer, it will make cycling more enjoyable.

BIKE SHOP ETIQUETTE (298-313)

298. Really good bike shops are at the heart of their local cycling community; some organise group rides and events, they are more than just shop. It's worth checking out your local store.

299. If you aren't mechanically minded, a good relationship with a local bike shop can really help you out!

300. Bike shops are an invaluable source of good advice; most shop staff are passionate about cycling and only too happy to share their knowledge.

301. Be a good customer – small, friendly bike shops often spend a lot of time with customers for very little return. If you just want to go in and chat about your bike ride at the weekend, at least buy an inner tube or take them all some cake!

302. Do not under any circumstances spend hours test riding bikes or trying on kit then go and buy it cheaper online. It's just not cool. Yes, it might cost more, but the advice from an expert and after-sales support is worth the price.

303. But online prices are cheaper. Yes, it's a tough conundrum. You might want to support your local bike shop but, well, money is money. When you add up the benefits – no delivery charge and a possible free fitting or a free service down the line – is it still cheaper? If it is, at least give them a chance, show them where you can get the product cheaper online and see if they will discount.

304. Some online retailers are selling products below the minimum recommended sale price and bike shops just can't match that (this is an issue the bike industry needs to sort out). A couple of shops I know have been happy for customers to buy online and then pay the bike shop a fair price for fitting, which seems to be a reasonable compromise. Ask if that is an option.

Trust a good bike shop to look after your pride and joy. © *John Coefield*

Good wheelbuilding is a 'true' test of a bike mechanic's skills!   © John Coefield

MAINTENANCE (162–313)

305. When I worked in a bike shop, the only customer we ever hid from was the one who started every conversation with 'I'm an engineer', then went on to explain why the latest gear ratios, frame geometry or bottom bracket design was completely wrong. Is this a tip? I'm not sure. Just don't be that guy.

306. Flicking the gear levers on racked up bikes when you are browsing is intensely annoying. It's the bike shop equivalent of tyre kicking.

307. Not all bike shop staff are amazing. I've come across wannabe pro-racers working weekends in bike shops who feel it is their sole duty to patronise you and reinforce that they are the 'real' bike rider, and you are wasting their precious time by even being in a bike shop. Just leave. There are enough amazing people working in the bike trade that you don't have to put up with this. As an aside, a female athlete posted the story of when she went into a bike shop to buy some flats for her commuter bike. The staff member selling them told her how she'd be much better off using clipless pedals to which she airily replied, 'Oh yes, I know all about them, I used clipless pedals when I rode in the Olympics last year.'

308. Clean your bike before you take it in for a service. Some shops now charge if they have to clean a really dirty bike and that is fair enough.

309. Bike shops are generally busy with waiting lists for bike services. If you enter a race or sportive months in advance, then you can also think ahead and get your bike booked in with plenty of time to spare.

310. Before going into a shop to buy something new, do a bit of research. It will help you get the most out of the advice you are being offered and help make sure you aren't being bamboozled by cycling sales-speak.

311. If you are going in to buy replacement parts for your bike, go prepared with the brand, model name and year of production.

312. Take a picture of the part as it is on your bike – this can help find an alternative replacement if the correct part is out of stock.

313. Many shop mechanics now run courses to teach you how to do the basics safely at home. This keeps a good relationship with your shop mechanic and extends your own skills.

Cycling the coastal roads of Cornwall, England. © *John Walsh*

From the train to the workplace: using a folding bike to commute in Leeds, England.   © *Joolze Dymond*

003

CYCLING LIFE (314–443)

'You know you are a cyclist when the bike on your car is worth more than the car itself.'

Riders at a Crimson Performance Road Race, England.   © Pete Aylward, RunPhoto

CYCLING LIFE (314-443)

SADDLE SORES (314–327)

314. To spare any blushes, this is a good time to remind everyone not to wear pants with their cycling shorts!

315. Even if you don't normally get a problem with saddle sores, hotter temperatures, rain or long days can leave you sore.

316. How stable you are on the bike has a huge impact on saddle comfort. However good your position is, your stability can make the difference. If you are rocking and moving and your weight is just dumped on the saddle it can lead to soreness.

317. Personal hygiene is critical in preventing saddle sores, but make sure you don't wash too aggressively or with too harsh a soap, as our natural skin oils also act as an emollient.

318. Sometimes you need to give your bottom a break. If you have sore or broken skin it needs time to heal; if you don't always take the rest days you need, this will have an impact.

319. Finding the right chamois cream is important – you want one with a good emollient factor that offers lots of long-lasting lubrication.

320. When it comes to the placement of chamois cream, it needs to be smeared across your perineum and areas that contact the saddle.

321. However, we female riders need to exercise a bit more caution about the type of cream we use and where it ends up (avoid anything heavily scented as it can be an irritant).

322. Regardless of genitalia, I strongly caution against mixing up chamois cream and embrocation.

323. And on that note, always do your chamois cream before you apply embrocation or warm-up balm to your legs. Once done, never forgotten.

324. Finally, on a similar subject, if applying a cream such as Savlon to a sore make sure you don't actually apply toothpaste. Your room-mate will be alarmed by the yelps of pain coming from the bathroom if you do.

325. If you have saddle sores then checking your position is the best place to start; once your position is right you can work through the other things such as shorts, chamois cream and saddle choice to make sure they are right too.

326. On the other hand, if you have tried everything else and still have saddle sores then it is time for a bike fit!

327. As my friend and bike-fit guru Phil Burt says, 'Bike fits are expensive, but they are not a luxury; think how much money you can throw away on fancy creams, shorts and different types of saddles without finding a solution for saddle sores.' As the former Head of Physiotherapy for British Cycling, and having spent five years with Team Sky, he knows what he is talking about.

CYCLING LIFE (314-443)

On the Pennine Bridleway above Todmorden, England. © John Coefield

BODILY FUNCTIONS (328–346)

328. Cycling can be a very visceral sport; blood, sweat and tears are an expected part of racing, but also snot, wee and worse.

329. Exercise-induced rhinitis can be a problem – this is the medical term for that annoying runny nose you get when you exercise. Up to 75 per cent of athletes experience a runny nose without any other obvious cause such as hay fever or a cold. That's a lot of snot …

330. Blowing a well-aimed snot rocket is one of the less than pleasant skills that cyclists acquire, but it has its purposes. It is much better than inhaling back up into your lungs or covering your gloves in snot trails. It's gross, you wouldn't do it on the street, but it seems universally accepted when cycling (though possibly less so post-Covid). Cover one nostril tightly, aim and blow.

331. When riding in a group, if you need to clear your nose check the wind direction and drop to the back or side to aim your snot away from other riders.

332. If you watch professional road racing, then you have probably seen a camera accidently catching a rider peeing while being pushed along by a teammate. It's a useful skill in a race but not one to use on the club run. As with snot, check wind direction before releasing the flow.

333. Cycling clothing designers have spent an inordinate amount of time trying to solve the problem of how women go for a wee in bib shorts. Many solutions are completely over-engineered and create more problems than they solve. Whether you go for waist or bib shorts is a personal choice. I prefer bib shorts; there is less pressure on your tummy, which is a performance issue, and fewer ugly bulges, which is a vanity issue. In summer, going for a wee is simple – just take off your jersey and drop your shorts. I timed a wee once to check this – two minutes. If I'm riding my bike for an hour or more, I'd rate the comfort of the shorts over the convenience of a quicker pee-stop. OK, rant over.

334. Male riders – if you ride in a mixed group, please be patient and wait for female riders if they need to stop. While you just whip it out, we have to go on a cross-country hike to find a convenient bush, so it takes longer.

335. When racing in the rain it is sometimes quicker and easier just to go in your shorts. I know a lot of racers who have done this, myself included. Always make sure that the rain is sufficient that the wet patch won't show. Only do this in extremis as your saddle and shorts will never recover from the experience.

336. On a night ride, if you go off to find a convenient bush remember to switch your helmet light off. I once made a spectacle of myself by effectively spotlighting myself while going for a wee.

337. Male riders – if you have a helmet mounted GoPro please switch it off before going for a wee, otherwise we will all be treated to 30 seconds of you looking down at your hand as you hold your member. (This really happened. Even worse, the guy in question had hooked his camera up to a TV screen in a bar so we could all watch it with our post-ride beers.)

338. Number twos are sometimes needed mid ride, often a long way from a toilet. If you have to go, you have to go. But please be discreet and move away from anywhere it might be found or trodden in. If you can, dig a hole and bury it or at least cover it.

339. In the absence of toilet roll don't use the Buff your girlfriend loaned to you. It's 20 years ago and I'm still bitter about it.

340. Never pick up a cycling cap found by the side of the road after a pro race; it is likely to have a little present in it.

341. A Mooncup – or another similar product – is a really good way of handling a period on long rides. You can keep them in longer than a tampon and they are much less likely to flood-out. Also, they're good if you're cycle touring or wild camping, as there is no waste to dispose of.

342. Lots of female riders notice points in their cycle where they feel strong and points in their cycle where they feel less skilful on their bikes. It's always been anecdotal, but there is beginning to be more research into the effects of hormone changes on female athletes. If you are a menstruating athlete, record the information in your training diary to spot trends. You can use this knowledge to improve training plans and even plan performance peaks.

343. Cycling through pregnancy is really just about how comfortable you feel. Unless you have complications, most midwives are supportive of cycling during pregnancy and advise you to 'listen to your body' and 'stick to what you are used to'. Recommendations for exercise suggest keeping to a low effort level, hydrating well and not overheating.

344. In pregnancy, I found men's bib shorts gave good bump coverage and allowed me to cycle in padded Lycra shorts all the way through.

CYCLING LIFE (314–443)

345. Adjust your bike and riding position as your pregnancy progresses. A more upright position leaves more space for your growing bump and also removes pressure from the front of your pelvis, which some women find uncomfortable as pregnancy progresses, when the pelvic joints start to move and ligaments relax.

346. I know a woman who cycled up until the day before she gave birth; I even know a woman who cycled to get her membrane sweep done when she had gone past term. I also know women who stopped cycling outside as soon as they got a positive pregnancy test. Everyone's experience of pregnancy is different. Do what feels right for you and your baby. Your bike will be there waiting for you when you are ready.

SHAVING (347–356)

347. Do you need to shave your legs to ride a bike? No, of course you don't, but you might like to. You'll hear loads of reasons for leg shaving: massage, reducing infections after a crash, aerodynamics. All of these have some truth in them, but you either like the look and feel of it or you don't.

348. Interesting fact: male cyclists started shaving their legs before women. Women only started shaving their legs in the first half of the twentieth century, a trend that was reinforced during World War II when there was a shortage of nylon stockings.

349. If you are really hairy, trim it down to a manageable length before wet-shaving, otherwise it will take ages and make a right mess of your bathroom.

350. For a close wet-shave you need a lot of lather. You can use anything from soap to shower gel or shaving foam. This helps the razor glide, gets close to your skin without pulling and keeps your skin soft.

351. Start at your ankles and work upwards in long, even strokes. Bend your knee to even out the contours and pull the skin tight, so you can work round it more easily, before switching to your thigh. Rinse and moisturise for that baby soft, just-shaved feel.

352. Where do you stop? At least a few centimetres above the line of your cycling shorts, just in case they ride up a bit and reveal a forest.

353. Advice from a male friend: don't shave your legs for the first time the night before a big race, as the silky feel of your legs beneath the sheets will distract you from sleeping.

354. Fake tan? Plenty do and no judgement here. After all, if you have gone to the effort of shaving your legs, you're damn sure you want them to look good.

355. If you are going for fake tan you can keep your tan lines sharp by wearing a pair of cycle socks and shorts and applying fake tan up to the line. I heard this from someone who is fairly well known in the cycling world, and they aren't the only one to do it. Not every pro gets their tan lines on training camps.

356. So far, we have talked about shaving legs, but if you shave above the short line there are other things to consider. Body hair provides a barrier between skin and the outside world, so a little bit of hair is a good thing. Frequent shaving or waxing can lead to inflammation of the hair follicles and make saddle sores more likely.

SECURITY (357–368)

357. No one wants to lose a bike to a bike thief. Lock up your bike somewhere visible. Look around for CCTV or street lighting that will act as a deterrent.

A rider at the Capernwray Road Race, England. © *Pete Aylward, RunPhoto*

CYCLING LIFE (314–443)

358. If there are other bikes parked up with parts missing or even a solitary back wheel, it's best to move on and find somewhere safer!

359. Be particularly careful around places like cafes where there are other cyclists and bikes. Canny bike thieves will turn up in cycle clothing to steal a bike unspotted.

360. Sadly, stealing bikes has become such an industry that thieves will follow cyclists on Strava to find out where bikes are kept. If you put up photos of you and your bike on any social media, but especially GPS tracking apps such as Strava or Garmin, be careful of sharing locations and make sure that you keep your privacy settings high.

361. Put your lock through the main triangle of your frame, not just through a wheel.

362. Try to position the lock so it is difficult to access and to limit the amount of working space around it.

363. If you have a long cable lock wind it round your bike, this makes it harder to use bolt croppers on it.

364. Use additional locks for wheels and take off anything valuable that could be easily removed.

365. Always lock your bike to something strong and im-movable so the bike cannot be lifted over it. I once saw a bike stolen from a metal fence – the thieves used the bolt cropper on the fence and took the bike with the fence still attached!

366. Use a Sold Secure bike lock – the industry standard for lock and security system testing. They come in four different grades, depending on the value of your bike, and are well worth the investment. Some insurance companies specify them.

367. This could feel a bit defeatist, but bike thieves are very determined so get your bike insured. It's not just the financial loss of your bike, but the frustration of missing rides or losing your transport.

368. Got a stable full of expensive bikes? Don't put them on your standard house insurance – your premiums will rocket! There are several specialist bike insurers who will insure your bike, not just at home, but also when you are riding, travelling and even competing.

TRANSPORTING BIKES (369–392)

369. This section is about travelling with a bike, rather than travelling on a bike. Using other forms of transport can help you see more places and explore further afield. Few of us have the time to start a round the world trip from our own back door.

370. When buying a new car, make sure your bike will fit inside it if you need it to. Seriously, take it with you and check.

371. You know you are a cyclist when the bike on your car is worth more than the car itself.

372. Most accidents involving bikes and car racks are down to user error. I worked for a bike shop that had a height restriction bar across the car park. Twice customers put their brand new bike on the roof of the car then smacked it straight into the car park barrier. Then sales assistants started to ask how customers intended to take their bike home.

373. When packing your car or van for a ride, never put your shoes, helmet, or anything else you may remove from your bike on the roof. Through bitter experience, I now have a rug I throw on the floor and everything gets placed on there before going back in the car.

374. Keep the disc brake pad spreaders you got with your new bike as they are really useful for keeping the brake pads apart while the front wheel isn't in place. Otherwise, fold up some cardboard and use that instead. If you don't do this and the brakes get accidentally squeezed, you will need to push the pistons back to be able to get your wheel back in.

375. Taking your bike on a UK train should be easy, but some rail companies seem to delight in making it hard. Nearly every train needs to be booked ahead – some of the more forward-thinking companies allow you to do this online or even on social media.

376. One of the biggest frustrations of booking travel with a bike is you often have to book your personal travel before being able to book your bike's travel. But if you can't take your bike you might not want to go. I have found myself stuck in this spiral of doom with more than one telesales person. If this happens, my advice is to give up and go with a different company.

377. From UK ports you can get on a ferry and take your bike all over Europe. Strolling on to a ferry as a foot passenger with your bike is an absolute delight. When you arrive at the other end you can just pedal away. It's a great way to start a cycle touring holiday – there is no need to pack and unpack your bike and you can enjoy a relaxed crossing instead of being cramped up on a plane.

378. If you travel with your bike a lot, it is worth investing in some way of packaging it. Specially designed bike bags and bike boxes offer lots of protection and make dragging your bike around airports really easy.

379. Bike bags are lighter than a hard case and the slight compromise in protection is made up for by being able to roll them up for storage. It's easier to squish a bike in a bag into a hire car than to try to play Tetris with a solid case.

380. Hard cases offer superior protection to bike bags, especially if it gets dropped from a great height, such as from the loading bay door of a plane on to a trolley below.

381. Bike bags allow much more room for ramming in all your cycle clothing and kit. You can just about get away with only one item of luggage if you fill your bike bag to bursting point.

382. A well-packed cardboard bike box – ask at your local bike shop for one – offers as good protection as some fancy bags and it can be recycled at your destination. Great if you want to ride away from the airport unencumbered.

383. Before packing your bike, make a note of all the measurements so you can replicate your position accurately when you put your bike back together.

384. Run a piece of electrical tape around your seat post where it meets the frame. Then all you have to do to get the saddle height right is to match up the tape with the frame when you pop your seat post back in.

385. Place a piece of white tape on your bars next to your stem and draw a line on the white tape to line up with the join between the front plate and stem (or other distinctive mark on your stem). This will allow you to get the rotation of your bars spot on when you rebuild your bike.

386. Pack a tape measure.

CYCLING LIFE (314-443)

387. Some people swear that bikes that are visibly bikes get treated better by baggage handlers; I can't say I've noticed a difference, but there is no harm in making it clear what is inside your bag.

388. Even if it is clearly a bike you are carrying you will get asked 'Excuse me, what is in your bag?' Tell them it's a dead body or a double bass. It gets boring saying 'a bike' after the third time. Obviously don't say this if the question is asked by actual airline staff rather than other passengers.

389. Always carry your shoes, pedals, helmet and one set of kit in your hand luggage. If your bike fails to materialise at the end of the flight you have everything you need to borrow or hire a bike. If you only have a week's holiday this can make a real difference to your cycling fun.

390. Every airport I have flown through seems to have different rules on what you can carry, even within the same country. Some places wave through gas canisters and multi-tools without a blink, others will confiscate them. Don't take your lucky multi-tool if you are going to be sad to lose it.

391. If you are taking energy drink powders, take sachets or decant into sandwich bags to reduce weight. However, if the luggage search reveals lots of little bags of white powder, you'd better hope that the customs official understands cycling.

392. Make sure you have any spares specific to your bike; for example, a mech hanger, the correct length and type of spoke or anything else unusual. With these things you can quickly and easily repair your bike; without them you can expect to waste your entire trip trawling round bike shops.

FINDING FRIENDS (393-406)

393. When you are on a bike you become part of the global community of cyclists; wherever you are in the world, cyclists acknowledge each other. It might not be more than a casual lifting of a forefinger from the handlebars, it could be a beaming smile and a wave, but having a moment of connection with a stranger feels good.

394. Bikes are great conversation starters – sometimes I watch the way cyclists check out each other's bikes and it reminds me of dogs circling each other to sniff under a tail.

395. Road cycling is by its nature a slightly location-less sport. Most cycling clubs tend to meet at car parks, lay-bys or local landmarks. Many times, as part of a club ride, I have met a random group of cyclists (often all men) at a bus stop and ridden off with them for the evening with no idea of who they are or where we are going. It is this that can make joining a cycling group for the first time a little bit strange. But club cycling is changing and increasingly clubs, both road and off-road, are realising that you need to offer a little bit more structure and a warmer welcome. Ask in your local bike shop or search for a local club on the British Cycling website, *www.britishcycling.org.uk/clubfinder*

396. You can ride side-by-side with someone for several hours a week, every week, and not recognise them when you see them in the supermarket. Do not use the phrase 'Oh, I didn't recognise you with your clothes on', especially if they are with their children or partner.

397. Conversations on bike rides are free-ranging and can often be deeper than those you might have in other social settings, even with complete strangers. It's something about the lack of direct eye contact, the rhythm of the pedals and the natural changes in conversational pace that allow people to reveal more and listen better.

398. Cycling is a great leveller – the mix of people you get on a bike ride is unlikely to be replicated anywhere else. Your job, the size of your house and what car you drive are all irrelevant. When it comes to cycling, 'let your legs do the talking'.

399. As well as making new cycling friends, you could try and persuade your existing friends of the joy of two wheels.

400. But ... just because you have fallen passionately in love with cycling doesn't mean your friends and family will, so go easy on the Lycra-clad evangelism.

401. Wait for a friend to say 'I'd like to try cycling, but ...', as that is your chance to offer solutions.

402. If you are helping a friend get into cycling, make sure they are safe. Check their bike over for them and do some gentle cycling together before heading out on the road or harder trails.

403. Make sure they are comfortable. Loan them kit. Make sure they have proper cycling shorts. Check their bike position.

404. If they aren't used to cycling, they will probably need to eat more than you. Keep up a constant supply of jelly babies and make sure they drink enough water.

405. If you are doing something new, it can make even the most confident person nervous – tell them about the route and offer little snippets of motivation all the way round.

406. Even if you are a 'serious' cyclist, to get your mate to come out again, you have to make it a fun experience for them.

These bikes are not worth more than the car. © *John Coefield*

CYCLING LIFE (314-443)

QUICK-WITTED ANSWERS (407-416)

407. When you start cycling, you hear the same glib comments, get asked the same questions and get accused of the same things over and over again. Memorise these and you will always have a quick-witted answer on the tip of your tongue.

408. Bike paths are optional. Yes, it is there; no, I don't need to ride on it.

409. No, I don't pay road tax, but neither do you. Roads are paid for out of local and national taxation. Road tax doesn't exist. And if you mean Vehicle Excise Duty, that is essentially a permit to drive a car on the road, it doesn't directly contribute to road maintenance. 'Road tax' was abolished in the 1930s for fear that it made drivers think they 'owned the road' – 90 years later they still think they do!

410. Cyclists are drivers too – so yes, we do understand. In England, over 80 per cent of people over 18 who cycle also drive.

411. 'Why are you holding up traffic?' I'm reducing the traffic. It's cars that cause congestion, not bikes.

412. 'Don't you worry that cycling is dangerous?' A recent study looking at long-term data found that, compared to commuting by car, commuting by bike was associated with a lower chance of dying from cardiovascular disease (24 per cent lower) and cancer (16 per cent lower). So, not cycling is more dangerous for your health.*

413. 'Shouldn't you be wearing high-vis?' In reported collisions involving bikes in the UK in 2018, the police, in a Department for Transport report, allocated the contributory factor of 'rider wearing dark clothing' to just three per cent of collisions.

414. 'Cyclists are always riding on the pavements, and they could kill someone.' Mile for mile, pedestrians are more likely to be killed by a motor vehicle than a bike. It's not bikes on pavements that pedestrians need to worry about.

415. 'Cyclists are always jumping red lights.' Between 2008 and 2018 cyclists in the UK were involved in four per cent of incidents where a road user (car driver/motorcyclist/cyclist) reportedly jumped a red light and a pedestrian was seriously injured. The other 96 per cent involved motorised vehicles. This was discovered by Freedom of Information requests to the Department of Transport by Cycling UK.

416. 'Are you riding in the Tour de France?' No.

CYCLING CAFES (417-427)

417. Does it have somewhere to put your bike? Or does it just have a picture of a bike somewhere? If it's the latter, it's not a cycling cafe.

418. Cycling cafes are a relatively recent 'thing'. Places where you get served by baristas whose knowledge of coffee bean roasting is matched only by their ability to recall the stage winners of every Grand Tour of the last five years. Before then, cyclists would go to charming little tea rooms, where you would have to jostle elbows with little old ladies and their china tea cups, or garden centres or greasy spoons. Less cool, but in many ways it was more relaxing. No need to strike a pose or talk loudly about your training plans or how many miles you had covered that morning.

* www.thelancet.com/journals/lanplh/article/PIIS2542-5196(20)30079-6/fulltext

Must have been some crash! © *John Coefield*

419. Avocado toast and macchiatos might hit the spot for a certain type of cyclist, but the best cycling cafes are ones that do all-day breakfasts and have plastic chairs, so you don't need to worry about having a wet bum.

420. Cycling cafes have opened the doors of cycling culture to people who aren't cyclists – yet. They pop in for a coffee and slowly, but surely, cycling starts to draw them in. It's a softer introduction than stepping foot into a bike shop for the first time. Bike shops can be very closed environments, but you don't even need to own a bike to go in a cycling cafe.

421. Location is everything when it comes to cycling cafes – for it to really work it needs to be in the right place in your ride. Two-thirds of the way round your route is perfect.

422. Cafes at the top of hills are fun. You can stir the competitive hill climbers into action and send them on ahead to get the order, then dawdle up at your own pace. Plus you start your ride again with a downhill.

423. At this point I should probably say something sanctimonious about being careful to only replace the calories burnt during the ride, and choosing foods with the right balance of protein, carbohydrate and a little fat that will digest easily and fuel your ride home. But we all know you are just going to have a massive slab of carrot cake anyway.

424. John Ibbotson, a much-missed cycling friend, taught me that 'Calories consumed while cycling don't count.' A hugely talented professional racer and coach, he was full of gems of wisdom, cycling knowledge and was a great cafe stop companion. If I'm ever in doubt about whether to eat cake at a cafe I just ask myself, 'What would Ibbo do?'

425. Coffee and cycling have a long cultural relationship. Many of the countries that take pride in their coffee also excel at cycling. Italian espresso machine manufacturer Fabbrica Apparecchiature Elettromeccaniche e Affini (or FAEMA), sponsored the eponymous Faema cycling team, launched in 1955, which included Belgian cyclist Eddy Merckx. And anything Merckx did was cool.

426. If you are going to drink coffee like a pro cyclist, it needs to be short, strong and black before your ride but post ride you can treat yourself to a latte or cappuccino, so the protein, fat and calcium in the milk can aid recovery.

427. This is the exact reverse of true coffee-drinking culture, where a milky coffee is for breakfast and never taken after 11.00 a.m.

CYCLING LIFE (314-443)

ODDITIES AND OBSESSIONS (428-443)

428. Cycling should come with a warning: 'May cause addiction.'

429. Bike riding will permeate every part of your life and influence every decision from what car to buy (will a bike fit in it?) to where you go on holiday (are there any good trails nearby?). It's not a bad thing, it is just the way it is.

430. Even if you aren't vain, at some point you will flex a calf muscle and feel a twinge of pride. You built that!

431. Road cyclists are attracted to shiny things like magpies – you won't be able to ride past a reflective shop window without checking out your position and pedalling action.

432. Checking the weather forecast becomes a daily, if not hourly, ritual, to make sure you time your ride for the best conditions.

433. Allow an extra 10 minutes to decide whether or not you need to take a rain jacket. You will do this before every single ride.

434. 'Look good, feel good' is a standard mantra of bike riders, but you can take the matchy-matchy approach to kit coordination too far. If your valve caps match the arms of your sunglasses you are either naturally a cycling fashion icon or totally obsessed.

435. If you can't go fast, look shiny.

436. If you are fast you don't need to worry about how you look.

437. 'Aero' has taken over from 'lightweight' when it comes to bikes and wheel design. The 'Weight Weenies' can return the scales to the kitchen and stop weighing their components, but the obsession with weight is deep-seated and lingers on.

438. Socks. Fashions for heights and colours may come and go, but the obsession with socks will always remain. Even the world governing body of cycling, the UCI, has enshrined sock height in its rule books.

439. The satisfaction in completing a ride without putting your foot down or cleaning a technical section without a dab has the same energy as when you were a kid and managed the walk to school without treading on a crack.

440. Cycling ruins the pleasure of walking. Even if you genuinely enjoy walking in the hills, there will always be one little trail feature or one great downhill section that will make you itch to have a bike under you.

441. Never stand when you can sit; never sit when you can lie down. Cyclists are the most supremely lazy of beings when not actually riding their bikes. Always conserve your energy for the one true purpose: cycling.

442. This is in direct opposition to what most of us really need, which is to eat less and move more. Unless you are training like a pro, you don't really need to rest like one.

443. This is a tip from the long-suffering wife of a mountain biker. As a super-dedicated runner herself, she totally gets sport but 'I don't need to hear every detail; I'm really happy you had a great ride and you knocked three seconds off a Strava segment but behind the smile and glazed eyes I'm actually thinking about what is for dinner.' There is such a thing as oversharing.

© John Coefield

Backcountry mountain biking above Briançon, France. © *John Coefield*

Sarah Rycroft on North Uist, Outer Hebrides. © *Stephen Ross*

004

DISCIPLINES
(444–588)

*'Racing means putting your ego on the line.
Be prepared for that. If you can win, you can also lose.'*

The segregated cycling 'Greenway' makes it a safe and enjoyable experience to cycle across Bradford, England.   © Joolze Dymond

DISCIPLINES (444-588)

COMMUTING, URBAN AND CARGO (444-460)

444. Who wants to pay to travel to work? Surely there are more fun things to spend your money on! Once you have made the initial outlay to buy your bike and kit, there is very little cost associated with daily cycle commuting.

445. If you are self-employed a bike can count as a company vehicle and if you use your bike for business purposes you can claim mileage, the way you would if using your own private car.

446. Cycling saves money on fuel or travel costs for you and reduces pollution and congestion for everyone.

447. One of the easiest ways to motivate yourself to cycle is to use your bike for transport, whether that is nipping to the shops or riding to work. It's a journey you intend to do anyway so gives a little bit of extra purpose to the ride.

448. Commuting by bike can form the basis of a really solid training plan without eating into your free time. If you live a rideable distance from work you are really missing out if you aren't commuting by bike.

449. Riding to work is made much easier by good preparation and logistics. Keep as much of the heavy stuff at work as possible, so you don't need to carry it every day, things like shoes and an outdoor jacket.

450. Have 'rest' days on Mondays and Fridays, so you can bring in all your clean clothes for the week on Monday and take them home again for washing on Friday.

451. Leave a spare set of clothes at work. The sinking feeling when you look in your empty rucksack and realise you are going to have to do the 9.00 a.m. meeting in full Lycra is best avoided.

452. Plan your route and ride it for the first time at a weekend, when the roads are quieter. You can take your time learning where to go without the pressure of getting somewhere on time.

453. As long as your general hygiene is normally good, baby wipes are a better-than-nothing substitute for a shower to get you through the day without offending your colleagues.

454. But even better, try and persuade your company to provide showers, changing facilities and cycle parking. Research has demonstrated that employees who cycle to work are more productive and have fewer days absent due to illness; encouraging cycling will benefit your employer's business.*

455. You can commute on any bike but choosing a bike that fits with your way of riding and your route will make riding to work more of a pleasure.

456. Two-thirds of all UK car journeys are less than five miles. This is a very easy distance by bike, and in congested cities the bike is probably going to be faster.

457. If you don't want to ride to work because it is too far, then consider an ebike.

458. If you don't want to ride to work because you might get sweaty, consider an ebike.

459. If you don't want to ride work because it is too tiring, consider an ebike.

460. Do you need to be able to carry groceries or even passengers? E-cargo bikes make ditching your car for a bike a much more realistic proposition.

* www.ncbi.nlm.nih.gov/pmc/articles/PMC5222872/

DISCIPLINES (444–588)

ROAD (461–472)

461. Any bike can be ridden on the road but road cycling as a discipline refers to the drop-handlebar, skinny-tyres breed.

> **462.** Road cycling is where some of the most arcane rules of cycling culture have originated. Whereas mountain biking originated in the 1980s, road cycling has over 130 years of heritage to draw on. Some of the things roadies say and do are well past their sell-by date but deeply embedded in the sport.

463. Despite the generally poor standards of cycling infrastructure, the difficulties of congestion and the fight for road space, there are still many amazing places to cycle on roads in the UK. Grab a map, get a good guidebook, check out the Sustrans long-distance routes and start exploring.

464. Until you started road cycling you probably didn't have very strong feelings on types of road surface, but that quickly changes. I admit to being slightly obsessed; I even have photos of my favourite roads. The sensuality of gliding along on buttery-smooth tarmac is the stuff of cycling dreams.

465. A thin strip of sinuous black-top winding its way around a mountainside is the road cyclist's equivalent to singletrack.

> **466.** You can waste hours and hours looking at aerial maps then dropping in Google's yellow man to explore a beautiful road from your desktop.

467. Road cycling covers a number of diverse cycling styles. From touring to racing, time trials and sportives, they all take place on the road. Each genre offers its own specialist bike, but a bog-standard ordinary road bike will do all of these adequately until you hit a level of interest or competition that makes you want to invest in something specific.

468. Being fast on a road bike takes incredible skill and nerve, but for some reason few road cyclists actively practise their technique. Good technique can help you go faster for less effort. Time spent honing your cornering or descending skills is just as valid as time spent working on your fitness.

469. Road cycling can be a very expensive sport (who am I kidding, all types of cycling can be very expensive), but you can get started on a budget. The market for very-well-looked-after bikes that are only two to five years old is strong, so check out eBay or your local marketplace for ways to make your budget stretch further.

470. Fans of road racing and road cycling like to sprinkle their cycling chat with French and Italian phrases; if your water bottle is a *bidon*, your local hill a *côte*, you consider yourself a *grimpeur* or you enjoy the *pavé,* then you have definitely caught the road cycling bug. However, if you start talking like this then your family and friends may cease to listen to your cycling tales.

> **471.** *Breaking Away* – released in 1979 – and *American Flyers* – released in 1985 – are my absolute go-to films for mindless entertainment with a cycling angle. If you haven't already experienced the joy of these two titles, give them a go. They are very of their time, but the cycling phrases and scenarios still ring true. I still maintain that *American Flyers* was the highlight of Kevin Costner's career, though I'm not so sure he would agree.

472. *Icarus*, which won the Academy Award for Best Documentary Feature in 2018, isn't just about cycling, but is an eye-opening insight into the often murky world of professional sport.

Bowderdale singletrack in the Howgills, England. © *John Coefield*

MOUNTAIN BIKING (473–485)

473. Off-road biking covers a huge range of cycling. From pedalling along a canal towpath, to short and fast uber-technical downhill racing, to climbing and descending huge alpine mountains.

> **474.** As bike technology develops, the type of terrain and riding each bike is designed for becomes more and more specific. It was a bit different 'back in the day' when riders would compete in both downhill and cross-country racing on the same bike!

475. It's not the complete definition, but let's try and explain mountain biking disciplines using inches of travel. The more inches of suspension the bike has, the more technical and downhill-specific the type of terrain it is designed for. How much the rider and the bike enjoy uphill cycling is another good way of categorising it.

476. *Cross country* (XC). Light bikes; short suspension travel; skinny, fit riders. In cross-country racing, technical climbing is as much a part of the course as the downhill sections. Riders wear tight Lycra. Occasionally called by the derogatory term 'dirt-roadies' – this is a little unfair as, in world cup events at least, the courses are technical and favour skill over fitness.

477. *Cross-country marathon* (XCM) is the longer-distance version of standard or short-course cross-country racing. The bikes and technical challenges are similar, but the distances for a day event are up to around 100 kilometres. Multi-day stage racing is also popular.

478. *Trail riding* takes cross country up a level, with a desire for more technical terrain and a willingness to take on bigger obstacles. Bikes are a little heavier and more robust, there is more suspension travel and the emphasis is on fun not racing. Skin-tight Lycra gets replaced by baggy shorts. This is the natural home of the 40-plus weekend warrior.

479. *All mountain* steps it up again. Bikes that fall into the all mountain category feature a good 15 centimetres of travel to cope with the steep drops, jumps and rocky sections you'd expect on a mountainside. Baggy shorts get augmented by knee and elbow pads; crashes aren't inevitable, but the technical terrain and riding style make the consequences greater.

DISCIPLINES (444–588)

480. *Enduro*, which is the most multifaceted of all mountain biking genres, combines the physical endurance of XC, the mental focus and skill of downhill and the power to climb. It revolves around racing; similar to a car rally there are three to six timed sections which combine a variety of technical challenges, including climbing, interspersed with neutral transfer stages where you have a limited amount of time to ride to the start of the next timed section.

481. *Downhill* (DH). Gravity rules when it comes to this – it's all about relatively short, incredibly challenging and technical descents. With no need to pedal uphill – there are uplifts for that – there are no weight worries so these long-travel suspension bikes are the heaviest and burliest you will find off-road without a motor.

482. *Freeriding*, as the name suggests, is mountain biking without rules. It's all about the creativity and the challenge of mastering trail features and man-made obstacles, from jumps and ladder drops to dirt jumps and scarily narrow log rides.

483. All of these genres have blurred edges and the cynical amongst you may be pointing at various bike manufacturers and marketing departments for creating divisions in mountain biking where they don't exist. Take it all with a pinch of salt.

484. When it comes to mountain biking, it is all about the bike (a bit). You would be foolhardy to attempt a downhill track on a cross-country bike.

485. Suspension technology is a bit of a skill compensator, just know your own limits. A skilful cross-country rider will be happy tackling descents on a hard-tail with no suspension that a less confident rider with 15 centimetres of travel wouldn't attempt.

GRAVEL (486–497)

486. Gravel bikes are a road–mountain bike hybrid, designed to give you the best of both worlds. They usually have dropped handlebars and fairly wide, knobbly tyres.

487. How you position your body on the bike is important to maintain grip and traction and to make sure you aren't thrown off-line by rocks, roots or gravel.

488. You won't be using the drops much; instead have your hands on the tops of the bars and move yourself further back on the saddle to increase your power and to help maintain stability. You will feel more planted and secure on the bike.

489. When you're riding on gravel, you don't want to feel like a passenger perched lightly on top of your saddle, you need a bit of muscle.

490. Drop your heels as you pedal to help push the tyres into the ground, increasing your traction even further.

491. Sitting further back in the saddle also allows you to make best use of your big, powerful glute muscles.

492. When you are gripping the bars tight a little cushioning will help your hands. Gel bar tape, or even a double layer of ordinary tape, is a good idea, but be careful not to increase the width too much as this in itself may cause strain.

493. A cheaper solution is to wrap your bars with an old inner tube, don't pull it tight too much to allow some cushioning, then put your ordinary bar tape over the top.

494. High cadence, light pedalling can allow you to bounce more in the saddle. On loose gravel, through mud or over rocks you might find a lower cadence better.

Endurance cyclists and GB Duro finishers Josh Ibbett and Gail Brown on the Further East route, East Anglia, England. © *Markus Stitz*

Riders at the Cyclo-Cross National Trophy series, England. © Pete Aylward, RunPhoto

495. Lower cadence and harder gears also help to pull you down into the saddle and encourage a strong, stable position.

496. The more speed you have when you hit a challenging section, the further you get before it starts hurting! It is easier to keep it rolling in a bigger gear.

497. Before employing the 'attack with speed' approach, hone your front-wheel lift. Hitting anything hard with your front wheel is a quick way to an exit over the handlebars.

CYCLO-CROSS (498–514)

498. Cyclo-cross originated as a way for road racers to keep their skills and fitness sharp while satisfying their competitive instinct through the winter months.

499. Cyclo-cross is an excellent way of maintaining your summer fitness through to next spring. It's also a discipline in its own right.

500. It is one of the best and most bonkers ways to race a bike. Cyclo-cross also has the best fans. Beer, brass bands and busloads of supporters make it one of the most enjoyable of all cycling sports to watch.

501. Cyclo-cross-specific bikes are not dissimilar to road bikes. They have a little bit more clearance for mud, slightly more relaxed geometry for better handling off-road and no bottle cage bosses so the bike is comfortable when you are carrying it on your shoulder.

502. Sorry, did I forget to mention that? Cyclo-cross races always have a section where you have to shoulder your bike and run.

503. Short races and twisting courses mean that you can see other riders multiple times per lap. There are plenty of oooh and aaaah moments as competitors slip and slide in mud, elbow each other off-line in the corners, power their way through sand and showboat by riding up flights of steps and hopping multiple sets of obstacles.

504. Cyclo-cross is one of the most accessible types of racing. Because courses are short, you are never going to finish more than a handful of minutes behind the winner, even if they did eight laps to your four. At local league events, you can race on mountain bikes, you won't need a licence and you are guaranteed to have a lot of fun.

505. If you get into cyclo-cross seriously, you will start wanting a second bike, as you can swap your bike in designated pit areas where your willing helper will wash it or fix it ready for you to collect on your next lap. It starts to get expensive when you are buying two of everything!

506. Cyclo-cross will make you fit, no doubt about it. The fast pace and repeated accelerations out of dead turns, across energy-sapping terrain and up steep hills mean that over the course of a 35- to 60-minute race the intensity level barely drops.

507. Cyclo-cross courses require high levels of bike control and skill. They feature many tight turns, short, steep climbs and changes in surface. To remain fast and smooth through all of these challenges you need to be constantly shifting gear and adjusting your cadence. A bad shift and loss of momentum might mean you have to run a hill where you could have ridden; a dropped chain will almost certainly lose you places.

DISCIPLINES (444–588)

508. Riding cyclo-cross teaches you how important shifting your weight around the bike is for maintaining grip, holding a fast line or lifting your wheels off the floor to clear an obstacle.

509. If you are more used to perching on top of your bike and maintaining the same position throughout your ride, then cyclo-cross racing will teach you some useful skills in bike handling. You will quickly learn how to use muscle and body weight to control your bike and throw it around.

510. Fast cornering isn't necessarily something you want to practise on hard tarmac. If you are learning about how far you can lean your bike and how fast you can exit a bend, it is much better to experiment on a soft, muddy surface!

511. Cyclo-cross encourages you to try different lines and to look at the surface of the inside of a turn for where you can get most traction. It teaches you how to adjust your speed and how to judge the best entry and exit points of a corner. Riding in slippery conditions teaches you to stay loose and relaxed on your bike and, if it does start to go wrong, how to recover it.

512. An increasing number of events are taking the fun and daftness to even greater heights. The fancy dress Halloween Cyclo-Cross at Herne Hill Velodrome has a course designed to allow a maximum amount of showing off, with mountain-bike-style gap-jump and rhythm section features. The Rapha Supercross events include the tequila shortcut, which allows riders to shave seconds off the course by downing shots.

513. Cyclo-cross is already a ridiculous sport. You are racing off-road on a completely unsuitable bike, but it just seems to spur riders on to even sillier things. Course designers, when not constrained by UCI rules, add ridiculous challenges like the 'spiral of doom', where you circle all the way in, only to dead turn and circle all the way back out.

514. If this doesn't sound serious enough for you, not like 'proper' road-racing, you might want to look at where the top roadies du jour got their skills. Mathieu van der Poel, Wout van Aert and rising UK star Tom Pidcock can all be found circling muddy fields in winter.

EBIKES (515–524)

515. Don't knock ebikes, they are brilliant. They make cycling more accessible, they allow riders to explore further and they help push people to discover new cycling experiences.

516. Even if you don't need an ebike, you might enjoy riding one.

517. Ebikes make replacing a car with a bike a much more realistic proposition. Particularly if you get an e-cargo bike. For the same amount of physical input, you can travel further and faster, making longer commutes and more challenging gradients completely possible, even on a daily basis.

518. If you think you live too far from work to commute by bike, or that riding to work would be too hard for you, an ebike allows you to think again.

519. You'll hopefully remember to charge your ebike battery, just don't forget to charge your own! The motor is taking some of the strain, but you are still contributing. Cyclists run on food and water (and cake and coffee).

520. To build fitness you need to do large amounts of easy exercise. Riding an ebike with pedal-assist lets you get your heart rate into a zone where you are building fitness and burning calories with the added benefit of being able to go further and faster than you could under your own steam.

Ebikes make local journeys achievable for all, wherever you live. © Joolze Dymond

521. Different modes are there to support your cycling when you need it; using your ebike's pedal-assist will help you ride further and more often, so don't feel guilty about using assistance

522. Using your ebike's modes correctly will help you get the most reach from one battery charge.

523. The majority of your riding on the flat will be in eco mode – this means you are doing more of the work and your ebike is contributing just enough to make cycling feel easy.

524. When you get to a hill or more challenging terrain, it's time for boost. It gives you an extra push, but you are still working – it is not a free ride to the top!

FAMILY CYCLING
(525–538)

525. Getting the whole family on two wheels is brilliant for having fun together. It can be useful for transport, as little legs will often pedal further than they will walk and it's a positive way to introduce children to an active and healthy lifestyle.

526. There are many ways to carry small children by bike. The method that works for you depends on a lot of things, including your own bike confidence, how far you have to cycle and what other activities you need to do as well.

527. Bike trailers are really versatile, as you can accommodate more than one child and many of them allow different attachments to make them usable for other sports. When you can convert your bike trailer into a running buggy, cross-country ski-sled and pushchair, you've got no excuse for saying having a child has put a stop to adventures. (But they do definitely change them.)

528. Bike seats give children a feel for riding a bike, they can have the wind in their hair and you can chat to them throughout the ride, which is hard to do when they are in a trailer. Front-mounted child seats are increasingly popular as it is easier to communicate, and they are sat within the protection of your arms on the handlebars, which some children and parents prefer.

529. Some children take to their bikes with virtually no persuasion, but others need time to develop their interest. Leave their bike somewhere they can see it and play with it, even if they can't ride it, to build familiarity.

530. Offer the bike as an option every time you go out or to the park. When they are keen, encourage them, but don't make a fuss if they don't fancy it.

531. The age of stabilisers is over; learning with a balance bike has revolution-ised the way generations of children learn to cycle.

532. Using a balance bike, a child builds the confidence to lift their feet off the floor and glide so they can start to understand how to control their bike with slight body movement before adding the complication of pedals.

533. Once they have the balance nailed, it's much easier for a child to get to grips with pedalling, as they have already learnt the fundamentals of balance and steering.

534. Learning to ride a bike inevitably involves falling off at some point and the fear of falling off can become a barrier for some children. Watching your child fall off can also upset a parent. Just remember how many falls they had to do before they could walk.

535. Once your child can pedal, it will be the first time that they can move away from you quicker than you can run after them! As liberating as this is for a child, it can also be daunting for them and for parents.

536. Teach children how to use their brakes properly from the start. Brakes should be squeezed slowly, not suddenly pulled on. Encourage your child to keep their fingers resting on the levers when holding the handlebars, so they are ready to squeeze the brakes when needed.

537. You can build road safety awareness even before your child is cycling on the road. Get them to spot the colours of traffic lights and talk through what you are doing when you drive or cycle together. Ask them to count the number of bikes or red cars they see so they are paying attention to what is around them.

538. When cycling with your children on the road, the best place for you to ride is slightly behind and to the right of them. This allows you to protect them from behind and clearly see what is going on in front of them so you can communicate instructions if need be.

TOURING AND BIKEPACKING
(539–549)

539. Nothing beats cycle touring for the feeling of total freedom. Your bike and your belongings become your little home on wheels. It is both transport and accommodation. You can go where you want, when you want. Total self-sufficiency. No one to answer to but yourself and the road. If you want to get away from the restrictions of everyday life, this is the way. You will feel the stress peel away with every pedal stroke you take.

Balance comes first before pedalling. © Hannah Reynolds

540. Touring covers every self-sufficient ride that includes an overnight stop – so that can be anything from a weekend away to months, or even years, on the road or trail.

541. A bicycle is a passport to discovery; with a bike you can head off the beaten track and immerse yourself in unfamiliar landscapes and culture. A bike can take you deeper into a country's heart and soul, it can take the rough paths with the smooth and spark conversations and connections with the people you meet.

542. Travelling by bike is a sensuous experience, it brings you in touch with the terrain, you can breathe in exciting new aromas and taste new foods. From your saddle you can get closer to nature and wildlife, seeing more than you can from a tour bus window.

543. Travelling by bike is fast enough to see changes in scenery and culture, even over the course of a day, but slow enough to absorb it and take it all in. The best way to experience any new place is from the saddle.

544. Exploring by bike offers a freedom and independence that no other form of transport does. You are not confined to timetables or even routes. While the hoards flood one pictur-esque village, snapping away and waving their selfie sticks, you can pedal your way to the next one, the one off the beaten track.

545. Forget time when you are touring, put your watch away and switch off Strava. It doesn't matter if 100 kilometres takes you a day or a week. It's the experience that matters.

546. Cycling away from your own front door is a brilliant way to start a holiday. Even when starting off on familiar roads and trails, by about lunchtime on the first day you will be into new territory. You don't have to go far to experience something new.

547. A low-key way to try cycle touring could be as simple as cycling to a pub a decent distance away, stopping overnight and riding back the next day. All you need is a rucksack and a change of clothes. You can do it in a weekend, but it will feel like an adventure.

548. On long tours, scheduling in a luxury night can make all the difference to how you feel. A long hot shower and big comfortable bed can really refresh body and spirit. Don't worry, it won't make you turn soft; the lure of a breakfast buffet will get you out of bed in the morning.

549. Nothing makes you hungry like cycle touring. I don't know if it is the extra weight on your bike, the constant but low level of exercise or simply that one of the greatest pleasures of being on tour is stopping for food! Whenever I have done long tours I have always been ravenous. In the French Alps I managed to put on a stone in weight, despite riding over 150 kilometres every day. I blame the Brie.

RACING OF ANY SORT (550–566)

550. Racing means putting your ego on the line. Be prepared for that. If you can win, you can also lose.

551. Racing can cost you anything from a few quid for a club-level evening race to hundreds of pounds.

552. Once you start factoring in travel costs, racing can be a really expensive hobby, but it's also a great way to see new parts of the country and the world, while making new friends.

553. You can 'race yourself fit', but you need to have low expectations of how you will perform in training races.

554. When I lived in South London and had no commitments beyond work and bike racing, I would happily race in everything from club time trials and track races to road handicaps and cross-country mountain bike races. I raced so much I had no time to train. In hindsight, I would have got better results if I had chosen my events more carefully and planned my training with more precision, but I had a lot of fun.

555. Racing is pure and simple; it is one of the most intensely focused experiences you can have on a bike. You can go full-gas and give 100 per cent effort, something that is impossible in training. The feeling of having got it all out, tackled every technical challenge and performed to your best is deeply satisfying, regardless of the race result.

556. In most short- to middle-distance races, you don't need to be totally self-reliant. In road races, cyclo-cross or time trials, there is either a pit crew, a support vehicle or the understanding that if you get a puncture your race is over anyway.

557. Some people use races as a justification for training, but it's the training they really enjoy. It's OK, you can let this one go; just enjoy riding your bike if racing doesn't do it for you.

558. If you are starting to think you are the king of Strava, have boasted about 'winning' a sportive or think that getting the town-sign sprint on the club run every week makes you a racer, it is time to pin a number on.

559. Doing a race leaves you nowhere to hide, it reveals the weaknesses in your fitness, your technique and probably most of all your psychology. It can be the motivation you need to work harder and become a better bike rider.

560. Don't save your best kit for race day. Everything has to be tried and tested in training.

561. Try all of your foods and energy drinks in training before your first event to be sure they agree with your stomach and you like the flavour.

562. Avoid the temptation to panic train in the final two weeks before an event. There is little that extra training can do to improve your fitness at this stage, but it can make you tired.

563. Fresh and a little unfit is better than well-trained but knackered.

564. Reducing your training load before an event is an essential part of being ready, but for many people it seems to leave the door open for insecurities, nerves and doubts to set in.

565. Staying off the bike can take more discipline than getting on it.

566. If doubts set in, look back over your progress in your training diary or Strava and look at all the sessions you have done. That is fitness in the bank.

SPORTIVES (567–577)

567. The cycling equivalent of running a marathon, courses range from around 25 to 200 kilometres, or even more. The challenge is to complete the distance and record a time. It's not a race (although it is to some people).

568. Sportives have helped loads of people get into road cycling and discover new places to ride and meet new riders. Thanks to marked courses, mechanics' vehicles, food stations and the hundreds of other riders, it's a fun, safe and supportive way to challenge yourself to either ride faster or further than you have before.

DISCIPLINES (444-588)

569. I think we might have hit 'peak sportive' in 2019, but who knows? There was a point when there were events running all over the country every weekend and some of the most popular areas – the Lake District, the New Forest and Surrey – had multiple events throughout the year, even multiple events on the same weekend.

570. Some sportives pre-date the UK popularity boom and are aspirational classics for many riders. In the UK the Fred Whitton Challenge, Etape du Dales and the Dartmoor Classic are three events that pre-date the current crop of sportives and are as hard, if not harder, than alpine sportives.

571. Most sportives in Europe are called *Gran Fondo*; a literal translation is 'big ride'. La Marmotte in the French Alps (which finishes on Alpe d'Huez), Maratona dles Dolomites in the Italian Dolomites and Quebrantahuesos in the Spanish and French Pyrenees are three that are worthy 'bucket list' events.

572. Which event is harder? Cyclists love to use phrases like 'epic', so establishing which is the 'hardest sportive of all time' is important to some people. Having ridden a lot of the big European and UK events here is my subjective opinion: riding in the UK is harder.

573. For comparison: La Marmotte (174 kilometres and approximately 5,000 metres of ascent) versus the Dartmoor Classic (177 kilometres and approximately 2,900 metres of ascent). On La Marmotte, there are long, hard climbs, followed by long descents when you can eat, drink and recover before the next climb. The Dartmoor Classic is like the proverbial saw blade: lots of short and spiky uphills with very little time for recovery on the descents. Having done both, my verdict is La Marmotte is more 'epic' – the views, the mountains, the sweeping descents – but the Dartmoor Classic was a much more painful experience!

574. Sportives are getting longer and harder. The standard distance used to be 100 kilometres, now many are pushing 200 kilometres and there are more multi-day events appearing on the calendar. It mirrors the trend in running, where ultra-marathon distances are growing in popularity. Pushing yourself to go further is really satisfying, but there is also something to be said for trying to ride 100 kilometres faster. Both are good goals and training for speed takes less time than training for endurance. An important consideration for the time-crunched cyclist.

575. I've had some great experiences in France doing little-known (outside France) sportive events, which are often run by the local council, the Mairie. The quality of rider at the sharp end is way ahead of many UK events, but the overall feel is friendly and relaxed. Being France, the food stations and post-event meal are also superior. At one event starting in Beaumes-de-Venise near Mont Ventoux, every entrant was given a full-size bottle of locally produced rosé. That sure beats yet another finisher's medal!

576. Sportives attached to races are a completely different experience. The feeling of following in the wheel-tracks of the pros and facing exactly the same challenges as them is unique. Imagine playing on Centre Court at Wimbledon against your Mum, or the five-a-side team from your local pub having a kick around on the pitch at Wembley! It just doesn't happen. That's why events like L'Étape du Tour and RideLondon will always be special.

577. Although *Gran Fondo* events in Europe are run as races with prizes and trophies, most in the UK are not. In an event, you can choose how you ride and there will be just as many people enjoying a relaxed day out as there will people pushing themselves to get the fastest time possible. Just remember to not let your ego get the better of you. It is not a race. Enjoy it for what it is.

Riders at the Capernwray Road Race, England. © Pete Aylward, RunPhoto

Gravel-type bikes can open up all sorts of adventures. © *John Coefield*

DISCIPLINES (444–588)

ULTRA-ENDURANCE (578–588)

578. Further, rather than faster, seems to be the growing trend in cycling events. Pushing yourself to the limit of your endurance takes you to new places, in every sense.

> **579.** Ultra-endurance loosely covers everything beyond 150 kilometres. That's a lot of ground. From 24-hour events and multi-day races to trans-continental routes and round the world challenges, there is no limit to where an ultra-endurance cycle event can take you.

580. Ultra-long-distance events bring an additional set of challenges. It's not enough to be fit and fast, you need the resilience to do it hour after hour, day after day. Digestive problems, saddle sores and joint injuries are common factors in the undoing of an ultra-distance rider.

581. A cast-iron stomach is as essential as rock-hard thighs for keeping the pedals turning. As the distances get longer, you cannot rely on the carbs in sports food and need 'real' food, with a mix of protein, carbs and a little fat.

582. On self-sufficient, multi-day events, everything from pork pies and entire packs of Jaffa Cakes to 2.00 a.m. Maccy D's become ride fuel.

> **583.** Few people talk about one of the biggest mental challenges of long-distance events – boredom. You need huge mental reserves to keep finding the motivation and the joy in relentless, vaguely uncomfortable monotony.

584. You don't need to be fast to do ultra-endurance rides, but the faster you are the more ground you can cover, or the quicker you can complete the distance, which ends the suffering sooner.

585. Ultra-endurance is a form of racing you can come to later in life and still be very successful at. While you might never hit the peak fitness and sheer speed of someone in their twenties, you will have the mental fortitude and experience to deal with the day-to-day challenges.

586. On ultra-distance events, there is nothing to say you need to start and finish in the same kit. Five minutes spent changing your shorts and reapplying chamois cream can easily be pulled back, as a comfortable rider is a faster rider.

587. Psychologically, a quick change of your shorts doesn't just feel more comfortable, it can help with splitting up the ride into manageable portions so the second part, with your new shorts on, feels like a fresh start.

> **588.** If you really enjoy climbing and suffering, 'Everesting' is an ultra-endurance challenge that doesn't require you to go very far. Recorded on Strava to complete the challenge, a cyclist has to ride the same hill repeatedly until they've completed 8,849 meters of elevation gain – the equivalent of climbing the world's highest mountain. You can even do a 'virtual Everest' on Zwift without even having to leave your own garage.

Sarah Rycroft on Harris, Outer Hebrides. © *Stephen Ross*

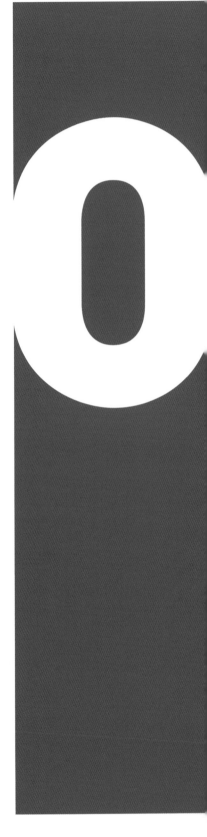

Riders at the Capernwray Road Race, England.　© Pete Aylward, RunPhoto

005

FITNESS (589-741)

'Doing something, pretty much anything, regularly is better than doing one really scientific, well-structured session only now and again.'

Cafes are an essential part of cycling culture.   © Hannah Reynolds

FITNESS (589–741)

ALL-ROUND NUTRITION (589–602)

589. Research into willpower has found various interesting things, but one of the most obvious is that good habits breed good habits. I find that if I'm riding well then I eat well. If I'm eating badly, I'm probably riding like it too.

590. Complete a good training session and you are less inclined to eat junk food. Sleep well and you have the energy for exercise. Be organised in your work and personal life and you will be able to carve out the time to train. Wow – that is just so easy, isn't it?

591. One of the hardest things about sport is that to deliver your best perform-ance you need discipline in every part of your life, from what you eat to how you sleep. But you can be a fit, healthy person and a good enough cyclist and still maintain a normal lifestyle.

592. 'Live like a pro' may make a great cover line for a magazine but for most of us it would be a very dull and one-dimensional lifestyle – and we'd still not be world-class cyclists even if we did follow it.

593. We all know a coffee helps us get going in the morning and keeps us awake when we are nodding off, but when it comes to riding bikes it does even more. It increases alertness, but it also reduces perception of fatigue and discomfort. We feel less tired, and cycling feels easier when we have had a coffee! No wonder cyclists get a little bit obsessive about their brew.

594. Carbohydrates are split into two groups: simple and complex. All sugars are carbohydrates, but not all carbohydrates are sugar. The more complex the carbohydrate the longer it takes to be processed by the body, resulting in a steadier release of energy. For example, starch and fibre are carbohydrates that release their energy very slowly. Simple carbohydrates, such as sugars, are absorbed more quickly giving a rapid energy 'spike' quickly followed by a trough.

595. Lots of us struggle with sugar cravings, we may even consider ourselves to be sugar addicts; the urge to reach for something sweet and sugary when we feel tired, down or lacking in motivation isn't unusual. This is often a sign that our overall diet needs to be looked at, as we aren't managing the peaks and troughs of energy release and are instead lurching from one energy spike to the next.

596. As with everything in life, it is all about balance; eating high-energy snacks while sat at your desk is both bad for your health and your waistline, but those same snacks eaten while on your bike are an excellent source of energy.

597. If you struggle with portion control, you have the best tools for the job at the end of your arms. Your hands are in proportion to your body size – they can help you get the right amount of food for your needs.

598. Make a fist – that's the right amount of carbohydrate in one meal.

599. Look at the palm of your hand – that is one serving of protein.

600. Put your hands together in a bowl shape – that is how much vegetables and salad to serve with your meal.

601. Traditionally cyclists loved a pasta party, but the danger of cramming in carbs the night before an event is that you overeat and then struggle with digestion. Increasing your carbohydrate intake in the three to five days leading up to an event will serve you better than a massive meal the night before.

602. Too much carbohydrate can lead to heavy legs the next morning.

EATING AND DRINKING ON THE BIKE
(603–622)

603. If you are riding hard for more than 90 minutes you will need to top up your body's reserves by taking on carbohydrates throughout your ride.

604. You can stop to eat or drink whenever you want if you are on your own or on a casual ride, but if you can't eat and drink on the go in an event you run the risk of either getting dropped or becoming dehydrated.

605. Remember that your water bottle has always been in the same place. You shouldn't have to look down to find it, nor to place it back in the bottle cage.

606. If you are right-handed, put your food in your right-hand back pocket for easy access.

607. Bonking, or blowing, is the cycling term for what runners might call 'hitting the wall'. Essentially it is when your body runs out of energy during a bike ride. Once you have blown you feel as if you simply cannot go on. When your energy levels have dropped this low it is very hard to recover and continue.

608. My worst 'bonk' was halfway up the Col de la Madeleine in the French Alps as it started to snow. My accommodation was on the other side of the mountain so I had no choice, not even to descend, and that would have been treacherous in the conditions. I was weaving around the road, then stopping and laying my head on my handlebars. In one of those moments I actually considered lying down in front of a car, so that the driver would have to stop and look after me. I eventually dragged my sorry arse to the top, found a cafe and ate everything in sight. An hour later I was over the top and into the next valley enjoying the sunshine, which tells you something about mountain weather as well as bonking.

609. Pacing plays a critical part in preventing the bonk – the harder you ride, the quicker you deplete your glycogen stores.

610. If you are wondering how much to eat, it needs a little bit of maths and some label checking. You can absorb 60 to 80 grams of carbohydrate per hour; this roughly equates to consuming a bottle of carbohydrate drink, half an energy bar and an energy gel.

611. Overeating can be as detrimental as under eating.

612. Dates are the natural equivalent of scoffing Haribo or energy gels. They are incredibly sweet as they are around 80 per cent sugar. The sugar in dates is usually glucose and fructose (with traces of sucrose and maltose), which ensures that you get a quick burst of energy and also a slow release over an extended period of time.

613. Bananas are nature's own energy bars. They are high in carbohydrate, easy to eat and digest, plus they come in their own handy packaging that doesn't create waste or damage the environment.

614. Bananas are interesting in many ways; their glycaemic index (how quickly the sugar in the food is absorbed into our bloodstream) changes as they ripen. A green banana is more fibrous and has a lower glycaemic index; a brown banana has a much higher glycaemic index, so releases its energy faster.

615. We are always being reminded to stay hydrated, but drinking to excess can lead to a condition called hyponatraemia, when the delicate balance of water to electrolytes (salts) in your body is upset. This can lead to severe illness and even death.

616. Thirst is the best indicator of how much fluid you need – drink at the first sign of thirst and stop when you feel you have had enough.

617. When it is hot and you are sweating a lot, the intake of electrolytes, such as sodium, becomes critical to replace the salts you are losing.

618. Using an electrolyte sports drinks can help address this, and so can eating salty foods along with plain water. A little bit of carbohydrate in your bottle, or as solid food, not only gives you energy, but also speeds up hydration.

619. On longer rides, or when working at higher intensities, your gut is more likely to be sensitive, so food you can normally happily tolerate will suddenly become a very bad idea.

620. Plan your nutrition and train with the food you will use during an event, so your body is allowed time to get used to it.

621. Nutrition includes the few days leading up to the event, what you eat on the morning and, of course, everything you eat during your ride. It will all make a difference.

622. If you can't stomach your usual breakfast food on the morning of an event, try making a smoothie of porridge oats, fresh fruit and milk or milk substitute that you can sip instead.

EATING AFTER A BIKE RIDE (623–635)

623. Easy, steady-pace riding can really rev up your appetite and it's very tempting to overeat when you get in! Often the appetite it creates is in excess of the energy burned.

624. Conversely, high-intensity training can suppress your appetite, making it harder to eat the food needed for recovery. This is where recovery drinks can be useful.

625. Stock your cupboards at home with easy to cook, healthy food so you can put together a meal quickly when you are tired and avoid the temptation to empty the biscuit tin.

Alpine MTB above Samoëns, France. © *John Coefield*

626. A very simple rule of thumb is to multiply the distance cycled (in miles) by 40 or 50 calories, so a 20-mile ride would need an additional 800 or 1,000 calories.

627. Remember to subtract the calories consumed on the ride. If you are fuelling properly (or eating carrot cake at the cafe stop) you may not need as many extra calories as you hoped.

628. The first 30 minutes after finishing exercise is known as the replenishment window, or glycogen window.

629. During this time your body is primed to be ready to replenish your glycogen stores and start rebuilding your muscles which have been damaged through hard exercise – all you need to do is give it the building blocks.

630. The golden ratio is 3:1, three parts of carbohydrate to one part of protein. The carbohydrate is needed to replenish energy stores in the form of muscle glycogen and the protein not only increases insulin production to help convert the carbs into glucose and drive it into the muscles, but it also helps to build and repair muscle fibres.

631. Bananas make a great recovery food for after a ride – add them to a smoothie or eat one with a glass of milk.

632. Keep it simple with Greek yoghurt, coconut water, berries and one banana. It's a perfect one-stop recovery drink with a blend of carbohydrates and protein.

633. Ice cream (yes, really!) makes a great recovery food.

634. If you are on the road, grabbing a chocolate milk from a petrol station is the best recovery drink you can get. It is easy to digest (for those who normally eat dairy) and contains exactly the right balance of fast-absorbing proteins from the milk, such as whey protein for muscle growth and repair, and slow-absorbing proteins such as casein, which gives your body protein building blocks to keep repairing over time.

635. A rough guide: for every kilogram of weight lost during hot-weather exercise, you need to drink 1.5 litres of fluid within the next two to six hours.

WORRIES ABOUT WEIGHT (636–648)

636. Firstly – you do not need to be super-skinny or light to ride a bike well.

637. Your power-to-weight ratio is undoubtedly a factor in race-level performance, but to obsess over this can quickly lead to an unhealthy relationship with food.

638. Professional cycling has some serious issues to address around body weight and body image. And where pro-sport leads, amateur sport follows.

639. When I was at a Q&A with a pro-rider on training camp, a member of the amateur cycling audience asked, 'How can I climb faster?' After looking her up and down, the painfully blunt answer from the pro was: 'Lose some weight.' This is the difficulty. Some weight loss will improve performance, but only if done safely and healthily, and it is the second part of this that is often forgotten in pursuit of the first.

640. If you have a body fat percentage of less than 12 per cent for a man and less than 20 per cent for a woman, then any more weight loss will be detrimental to your health and riding.

Summiting the Quiraing, Isle of Skye, Scotland. © *Stephen Ross*

641. It is also true to say if you have some fat to lose you will find that dropping a few pounds will benefit your speed.

642. Body fat is inert. To be totally frank, it is just lard, and the fewer blocks of lard you are carrying uphill, the faster you will climb.

643. Even on the flat, body fat makes a difference and, depending on how much you have to lose, it can affect your aerodynamics and your ability to hold a good riding position.

644. Fat loss needs to be done slowly over time so as not to compromise your health or your training.

645. If you want to lose some body fat, small incremental losses throughout the year are better than panic dieting to lose several kilograms in the spring.

646. Under-fuelling can have a big impact on your immune system. If you do a lot of endurance exercise you can be more susceptible to upper respiratory tract infections, so keeping the immune system supported is really important.

647. How much you weigh, how much body fat you carry and what you look like has no impact at all on your ability or right to have fun riding bikes.

648. Bananas should not only be eaten on your bike; the fibre in bananas called pectin helps to moderate your blood sugar levels and can reduce your appetite, making them a good snack between meals.

GETTING FIT (649–689)

649. When someone says they want to get fit, the next logical question is 'fit for what?'

650. Physiologist Dr Jamie Pringle, when talking about how to improve as a cyclist, used this great line: 'The secret to endurance training is doing enough, but not too much.' Of course, the hard part is knowing what is 'enough' or 'too much' for you.

651. When you feel great you want to do more and when you feel crap you want to do less. Sometimes this works out and you get fitter but more often than not it doesn't.

652. Doing something, pretty much anything, regularly is better than doing one really scientific, well-structured session only now and again.

653. People arrive at fitness in different ways, so generic training plans won't work for everyone.

654. If you really want to get fit you need a plan. There are a whole host of generic programmes to sign up to online; the better ones allow you to input personal factors about your available training time, current fitness levels, previous fitness levels and your strengths or weaknesses.

655. A training myth that keeps hanging around is that the *only* way to build your endurance is to do lots of long, slow miles.

656. Sprint training benefits nearly every type of cyclist. Even if your goal is a 100-mile sportive and you are very unlikely to ever find yourself sprinting for a finish line there are still clear reasons why it would benefit your fitness.

657. When you sprint, you recruit more of your muscle fibres to provide the maximum power to the pedals. During less intense efforts not all of your muscle fibres need to be engaged. You could say that sprinting hits the spots that other training misses.

658. If you're short on time but still want to be able to ride long distances, then sprint training (30 seconds of all-out effort followed by 4.5 minutes of recovery) has been shown to have similar benefits to endurance training. Try doing six all-out efforts in a 40-minute short, but tough, session. It's more painful than it sounds.

659. Sprint training also has a positive effect on your bike handling skills, reaction times and alertness. If you ride at one moderate pace for most of your training, you can start to feel sluggish and slow to respond – sprint training is a wake-up call to your whole body.

660. If you are new to sprinting or high-intensity efforts, then you are likely to get some muscle soreness and stiffness after your first few sessions, which is totally normal.

661. Sprinting increases the load on your ligaments and tendons so if a pain is sharp or located in one specific area, rather than a generalised ache, make sure you get it checked out.

662. Sprints are for everyone, road or off-road, whether you race or not. It's actually good fun and gives you a bigger hit of endorphins than a ploddy, one-pace ride.

663. If you never train fast you will never race fast.

664. *Power sprints* – from a slow start. This helps you to develop explosive power from a slow speed. Good for attacking, standing starts or on a climb. Get into a big gear and roll slowly till you are almost at a standstill. Either in or out of the saddle, accelerate and hold it for 20 seconds or until you start to spin out. Ease back into an easier gear and spin for five minutes. Repeat up to eight times.

665. If you are sprinting against other riders, then chances are you will already be moving fast. This helps you to accelerate to get the gap. Use a safe downhill slope to increase your speed; when you get close to the bottom of the hill shift gears and increase your cadence to accelerate. Keep the speed up as you hit the flat, or bottom of the next hill if it is a rolling stretch of road.

666. *Tabata style sprints* – repeated high-speed efforts with little recovery. One sprint is seldom enough in a race situation. This will help with repeated sprints out of corners or if you have to go again to make an attack stick. Sprint hard for 30 seconds then pedal easily for 30 seconds; repeat five times. Make sure you don't stop pedalling between efforts; you need to maintain momentum to keep the speed high. Recovery spin for five minutes.

Taking in the view from Curbar Edge in the Peak District, England.   © *John Coefield*

Urban MTB at Parkwood Springs, Sheffield, England. © *John Coefield*

667. Your position on the bike as the rider has the single biggest impact on aerodynamics and therefore speed. Next is your clothing and helmet, finally your bike and wheels.

668. Generally, road cycling is less hard on your body and less intense than mountain biking and off-road cycling. A simple rule of thumb is that one hour off-road is equal to two hours on the road.

669. Smooth pedalling technique comes from a strong, stable core. A popular analogy is that you 'can't fire a cannon from a canoe'. For your big, powerful glute muscles to fire correctly your pelvis and trunk need to be strong too.

670. Anything you do in the gym should be specific and transferable to cycling, for example working on split squats and single-leg squats. Before training with weights, it's a good idea to see a conditioning expert or physiotherapist with knowledge of cycling, who will be able to assess your posture and muscle recruitments, to get a personalised programme.

671. Everyone can benefit from basic body weight core exercises you can do at home. Every cyclist should be able to hold a plank, do body weight squats and press-ups.

672. Don't avoid climbs, even if you find them hard. This is where the biggest fitness gains can be made.

673. Focusing on your breathing is an easy way to relax your body as well as making sure that your muscles are getting the oxygen they need to power up a hill or ride hard on the flat. When we start breathing shallowly and fast, it sends signals to our brain that our body is under stress and in difficulty. Our shoulders tense up and our heart rate accelerates. Instead, focus on exhaling hard which will help your next breath go fully to the bottom of your lungs.

674. The traditional climbing face of a racer is somewhere between a snarl and a gurn, but something as simple as smiling can help you climb better. The action of turning the corners of your mouth up in a smile helps to relax the muscles of your jaw and neck which also sends messages to your brain that you are calm, relaxed and

in control. The added benefit of this is that everyone around you will you think you are super human as you smile your way up the climbs, barely registering any discomfort.

675. Our perception of a gradient changes from when we are on our own compared to being with friends. Crazy but true – scientists discovered that participants estimated the gradient of a hill as being less when they looked at it with a friend. If you find hills challenging, don't tackle them alone; buddy up with another rider and it will make the experience feel easier.*

676. As with any big task, reducing a climb down to smaller sections can make it feel more manageable. For instance, pick a point further up the climb, such as a tree, and focus on riding to that point. When you get there do something new, maybe take a sip of water or ride out of the saddle for five pedal strokes, then pick your next target.

677. Hate hills? Rubbish at climbing? Too slow? If this what you are thinking as you approach a climb it's time to change your tune. Talking negatively to ourselves can make us feel fearful – our body tenses up and we start to breathe more rapidly. We anticipate the climb to be difficult and we start expecting failure. Instead, turn it on its head: 'I love climbing', 'this is making me stronger', 'I am feeling good.' It might not sound much, but it works!

* www.ncbi.nlm.nih.gov/pmc/articles/PMC3291107/

FITNESS (589-741)

678. The more you do, the fitter you will get, to a point. Given that most of us can reasonably call ourselves 'time-crunched', any opportunity to ride a bike should be taken. If you aren't cycling to work already, it's time to get commuting.

679. Continuous, monotonous training doesn't allow for a steady build-up of volume and intensity; it doesn't lead to peaks in fitness and it doesn't allow for sufficient rest and recovery. Your body thrives on change – once you have adapted to one level of exercise stress you need to offer it something new.

680. You can't get fit without at some point getting tired. Fatigue is part of the parcel of training; simplistically speaking you do some training, it makes you tired, you recover from the training stimulus and your body adapts to it.

681. There are no rewards for who trains the most. The aim should be to do as little as possible to get a positive fitness adaptation.

682. Some people over-train, but even more people under-recover.

683. It is almost impossible to accurately predict what level of fatigue a given level of training stress will create. Your watch, heart rate monitor or swanky app does not have all the answers.

684. Lack of sexual arousal is a well known, but little discussed, anecdotal indicator of fatigue. I once interviewed a pro-rider on his training strategy and was told 'If I can't get it up in the morning I know I'm too tired to train.' Sadly, the quote got cut by a sub-editor.

685. If all else fails, buy speed (not that kind).

686. Investing in a fancy aerodynamic helmet, speed suit, fast wheels and a light aero bike will make you instantly faster. But it only works its magic once; after that, any further improvements need to come from you.

687. To really get fast and see long-lasting benefit from your investment, get a good coach.

688. If you barely have time to train, you definitely don't have time to train badly. Get a coach, or at least a training plan.

689. Remember – it is not about the bike, but it is sort of. When all else is equal between two riders, at the very top level of sport, technology makes a difference.

STAYING FIT (690-717)

690. Before you can look at marginal gains, you need to minimise the massive mistakes.

691. Why worry about shaving seconds off your times with an aerodynamic skin suit if your chain is dirty or stiff? If you really want to improve, take a big step back and look at the big holes in your fitness and preparation before examining the smaller details.

692. Seeing your fitness improving is amongst the most motivating things of all. Keep a diary of your training sessions and make sure you test your fitness regularly, so you can keep an eye on your progression.

693. Testing your fitness can be as simple as timing yourself up a favourite climb or regularly doing a favourite Strava segment.

694. No one can train for ever. You need to allow the time for adaptation, which happens during recovery periods – it is very important physically and psychologically.

695. Sometimes, to achieve the fitness progression you want, you will need to pause, or even go backwards in your training, before you can accelerate again.

696. A lot of fitness blogs talk about 'smashing your way through' or 'busting through to the next level', but that is as helpful as trying to knock down a wall by banging your head against it.

697. When success comes easily you might not realise that you are getting those results despite your bad technique, or your poor diet or training plan. But in the end those problems will limit your progression. If you stop progressing, you need to solve the riddle of what is holding you back and ultimately that knowledge and change in behaviour will be the key to making you a faster, stronger athlete.

698. A plateau forces you to try new things, examine your weaknesses and explore different ways to train. Take a couple of steps back so you can see the obstacle more clearly, look for the way round it and ask the experts; there are plenty of great coaches out there who will be happy to act as a guide to show you the route off your own particular plateau.

699. Following a training plan to the letter, regardless of any life issues, may feel like dedication, but ultimately it is the wrong choice.

700. Things that barely bother you when riding for two hours can start to be excruciating after five hours. If you have even the slightest niggle, your first port of call is checking that your bike fit is correct.

701. It would be totally naive to expect to ride 150 kilometres with little or no training, but it is much more manageable than you may think.

702. If you want to ride and survive 100 kilometres (rather than race it), you don't need to go beyond 80 per cent of it in training.

703. You can fake fitness during long rides and events. If you have a solid nutritional plan, pace yourself well, have great technique and ride clever you can get away with a lot more than your fitness suggests you should be capable of.

704. It's not all about physical fitness. Before a long, multi-day tour, get used to riding back-to-back days so that your bottom, as well as your legs, is ready for repeated days in the saddle.

705. Riding clever means not wasting an ounce of energy.

706. The single biggest energy expenditure you make as a rider is punching your way through the air. The less frontal volume you present to the wind, the faster you can go for the same energy output.

707. Simply riding on the drops, tucking your elbows in and lowering your torso will mean you can ride slightly faster.

708. Stop free-wheeling! Keeping the power applied to the pedals at all times will raise your average speed on a ride.

709. Stop braking (when you don't need to). Every time you touch your brakes you lose speed – obviously. Reducing how often you brake and learning to brake later will help you maintain your momentum. This is a skill that requires practice, but it doesn't require you to be any fitter. It is 'free speed'.

FITNESS (589-741)

710. Pro-cycling athletes have always been very careful about avoiding coughs, colds and viruses, even before Covid-19. British Cycling coaches teach their riders how to wash their hands properly and to open doors with their elbows – staying healthy is crucial to their training.

711. Hard exercise can leave your immune system suppressed and under strain; if you can, it is best to avoid busy, communal places in the hour after a ride when your body is most vulnerable. (This is the golden excuse for not doing the weekly shop or going to B&Q on a Saturday.)

712. Make sure you stay hydrated, as mucous is our natural defence against a virus entering our body. It will find it easier to get to work on your nose and throat if they are dry.

713. Taking vitamin C after bouts of exercise can prevent a cold. Higher doses at the onset of symptoms can reduce the length and severity of symptoms. Start taking it as soon as you notice symptoms. Be careful, as large amounts of vitamin C can cause diarrhoea.

714. If you have cold-like symptoms, follow these golden rules. For symptoms above the neck it is safe to continue with light training; exercise may even help to reduce symptoms and help you clear congestion.

715. For symptoms below the neck, and in particular if anything has made its way to your chest, stay off your bike completely until symptoms have gone.

716. Mental strength is more valuable than physical strength.

717. You can outperform your fitness, but if your head falls off in a ride or race it is game over, however good your legs are.

INJURIES (718-741)

718. Injuries can be broken down into traumatic and overuse ones.

719. Some traumatic injuries are hard to avoid, such as a car pulling out on you; however, a broken bone because you went out riding on an icy day can be prevented by intelligently considering the risks of going on the ride.

720. Overuse injuries rob you of training time and cycling enjoyment. Cycling should not be painful. There is no glory in pain and suffering from an injury.

721. Some problems respond well to rest, but don't be deceived by this. Chronic injuries never just disappear.

722. Riding for many hours in a fixed position will exacerbate any physical problems that you have.

723. That cycling is bad for your knees is one of the most persistent myths of cycling. While it might be one of the most common cycling injuries, it is not cycling per se that is the problem, but an issue in the way the bike is fitted to the body.

724. If you think cycling is bad for your knees, pitch up to your local running club and ask them how their knees are! Cycling places very little destructive loading on your joints compared to other sports.

725. If you are suffering knee pain, you need a two-pronged attack of bike fitting and physio to ensure, in particular, that bike fit and cleat positioning are correct.

726. If you feel pain at the front of your knee, the saddle is likely to be too low.

727. If you feel pain at the back or side of your knee, your saddle is likely to be too high.

Taking a spin around Lister Park, Bradford, England.   © *Joolze Dymond*

Forest trail at Sherwood Pines, Nottinghamshire, England. © *Rosie Edwards*

728. If you are feeling pain or tightness in your lower back, your saddle is likely to be too far back.

729. If your hands or wrists are hurting, or you're feeling numbness, your saddle is likely to be too far forward.

730. Numb hands are not normal. You may occasionally have hand numbness on longer than usual rides, but it should be transient and quickly alleviated by stopping cycling.

731. If you have constant hand pain, there is something wrong. It's normally a sign that you have too much weight on the upper body through a low handlebar or high seat height set-up.

732. A numb penis is not normal; it may be normal for you, but you don't have to put up with it. Gap saddles have been designed to relieve pressure on the pudendal nerve, which runs through the middle of the base of the penis and perineum.

733. On long rides, try riding out of the saddle for short stretches to relieve the pressure on your backside and allow blood flow to return; this is particularly important for preventing penile numbness.

734. If you get a burning pain in the ball of your foot, it is probably coming from the base of the first metatarsal or big toe. Moving the cleat backwards so the pedal spindle is slightly behind the big toe joint will decrease the loading and often resolves this issue.

735. There is no such thing as feeling 'good vibrations' if you are a long-distance endurance rider. Vibrations from your bike over time can lead to numbness, tingling and 'hot foot'. Anything that dampens it down, from inserts in your frame and frame design to gel handlebar wrap and padded gloves, will help.

736. Burning pain in your foot is sometimes called hot foot. If you are a sufferer, it might be time to give away your super-stiff carbon-soled shoes and swap them for something with a little more give and space, as feet can swell up.

737. I once took a hacksaw to the toe-box of a very nice pair of shoes to alleviate the pressure on burning, cramped toes. Extreme and not very stylish, but it worked. (Not all tips need to be followed.)

738. During your ride, don't be afraid to move around in the saddle – your riding position should be dynamic, not fixed, and moving around rests different muscles and relieves pressure. If you are on a drop-handlebar road bike, switch frequently between the hoods, tops and drops, as this will relieve hand pressure and give some relief to your back and shoulders.

739. Taking ownership of the cause of your injury and the process of recovery will help you understand your body better and make it less likely for you to be injured again.

740. Doing conditioning and rehabilitation exercises are a lot less fun than riding bikes, but they are worth it to fix an annoying problem.

741. The biggest predictor of injury in cyclists is having had a previous injury. Don't repeat things that have caused you injuries in the past; something has to change if you want to see a different result.

Rural cycling has its own unique hazards and challenges.   © *Hannah Reynolds*

Dust and blue skies in the Hautes-Alpes, France. © *John Coefield*

006

APPS AND TOOLS (742–825)

'When it comes to all training data, it is knowledge and interpretation that makes data meaningful. Data alone won't improve your training; it is what you do with it that counts.'

APPS AND TOOLS (742–825)

HEART RATE MONITOR (742–756)

742. A heart rate monitor shows your heart rate in real time and records it for later analysis. If you want to monitor your fitness and start training seriously, it is a very useful tool to have.

743. When you exercise, your muscles need oxygen. Your heart pumps oxygenated blood to your muscles, so the harder your muscles work, the more oxygen they need and the faster your heart beats. A heart rate monitor is essentially a rev counter for your body.

744. Heart rate monitors are relatively inexpensive and very accurate. While power meters are becoming the preferred tool for cycle training, heart rate monitors remain a training tool in their own right.

745. If you have a power meter you also need a heart rate monitor. A power meter tells you your output, but a heart rate monitor tells you how hard you are working to achieve that output. For the full picture you need both together.

746. A heart rate monitor can give you a lot of useful information about what is going on in your body, it is not just about how hard you are working while you are cycling. The more you understand about your body's response to exercise, the better you can tailor your training.

747. Resting heart rate, taken first thing in the morning before you even get out of bed, gives you a clue about what is going on in your body. It's all about patterns; if you see changes over several days it could indicate fatigue, illness or stress.

748. An athlete's resting heart rate can be as low as 40 beats per minute (Lance Armstrong claimed 32 beats per minute and 'Big Mig' (Miguel Induráin) 28 beats per minute). An averagely healthy, active person's is more likely to be 60 to 70 beats per minute.

749. Record your resting heart rate on your monitor for at least a minute, maybe two, without looking at it, to get an accurate picture. I used to be so excited to see if I was getting fitter that looking at my watch would send my heart rate up!

750. A heart rate monitor allows you to plan your training around heart rate training zones. Using training zones is the only way to accurately target the different components of fitness you want to work on. *(Table 1)*

751. Your maximum heart rate is the greatest amount of beats per minute it can reach. There are many formulas for estimating your maximum heart rate, the most commonly used is 220 minus your age. No formula is completely accurate; if you want to know your true maximum heart rate, you need to do an exercise test.

752. To find your heart rate zones you need to perform either a sub-maximal or maximal (max) test, where the effort level ramps up gradually until you can no longer meet the required pace. To do a test like this well needs motivation and commitment.

753. A max test done well nearly always results in going cross-eyed and throwing up. You are pushing your body to its absolute limits, so it is not something to undertake lightly. If you want to do something like this, it is best to do it under the supervision of a coach.

754. You can perform easier (and safer) sub-maximal tests using a heart rate monitor and a home trainer. Apps like Zwift, The Sufferfest and TrainerRoad have ones to follow.

755. If you are going to use heart rate data for training, it needs to be recorded and analysed. Data on its own is meaningless unless you use it to influence your training. The easiest way to make use of heart rate data is by uploading it to a tool or an app such as TrainingPeaks or Strava.

If anything, freak weather could give you *more* of a reason to get out.   © *John Coefield*

Cyclists on the Monsal Trail in Chee Dale, Derbyshire, England. © *Dave Parry*

756. With power, as soon as you press the pedals you get feedback, but with heart rate there is a delay while your heart rate adjusts to the effort. It is almost impossible to use heart rate for really short interval efforts. This is one of the reasons why, for really accurate training, a power meter and heart rate monitor work well together.

POWER METER (757–766)

757. Using a heart rate monitor and power meter together gives the strongest overall data picture of your performance. In the simplest terms, a higher power for the same heart rate suggests a training improvement, a lower power for the same heart rate suggests a loss of fitness and/or fatigue.

758. Power meters provide an absolute measure of your output. Unlike heart rate, power data is not influenced by heat, hydration, glycogen levels or fatigue. But this is also why heart rate and power data should be used together.

759. Your mood states give an indication of how your body is adapting to training; if you are feeling tired, or motivated, it is worth recording it in a training diary. As with heart rate, the more metrics you combine with your power data, the more complete the picture.

760. Power meters use strain gauges to get their data. You can buy power meters that sit in the bottom bracket, pedals or rear wheel. There are pros and cons to each design. As well as considering accuracy, it is worth thinking about how practical they are to use, particularly if you are swapping between bikes a lot.

761. Recording your data is the only way to make it useful. One session tells you very little, but over time the numbers start to give a really good clue and patterns begin to emerge.

762. Calibrate your power meter. If you are going to the effort of recording data, make sure it is accurate.

763. Metrics measured by ride data don't tell you everything about what went wrong on the day; fuelling, nervousness and your emotional state have an effect on power production and performance. Human beings are complex.

764. Data is emotionless – 'numbers don't lie'. Using data to make training decisions gives us a pleasing kind of certainty. If your power data says you didn't hit the numbers there is no arguing with it (but you should be trying to work out why you didn't).

765. Data alone has no power; it is what you do with it that counts. If you aren't changing or adapting your riding or training based on the data, then your computer is just very expensive handlebar decoration.

766. While a power meter will give you precision and accuracy, you can still monitor how hard you are going the old-fashioned way, using 'feel' and how able you are to talk and breathe. *(Table 1)*

GPS AND BIKE COMPUTERS (767–772)

767. The amount of information you can get on your handlebars is absolutely mind-blowing. We are a long way from those trip computers that needed a magnet on your front wheel and a few feet of wire to wrap round your forks and get stuck in your wheels. Incidentally, these are still available if you prefer them.

768. A bike computer can now have functions that include navigation, weather reports, speed, distance ridden, distance from home, elevation, altitude, VAM (a measure of climbing speed), power, heart rate, temperature and even virtual friends to race against. They can do *almost* everything, but they can't ride your bike for you. You are still the boss of that.

769. With so much on offer, think carefully about what you actually will use and need. This few moments of thought could save you a lot of money.

770. Forget for a moment about all the information and data the computer gives you; it is screen size and button size that can make the difference as to how easy you find it to use.

771. Forgetting to charge your computer is infuriating – but don't let it ruin a good ride. Even if you haven't recorded the session, your legs will still know you did the training.

Power zone	Percentage of functional threshold power (FTP)	Feels like	Training purpose
Zone 1	Less than 55 per cent	Light spinning	Recovery/warm-up
Zone 2	56–75 per cent	Chat freely	Aerobic endurance
Zone 3	76–90 per cent	One sentence	Tempo
Zone 4	91–105 per cent	Breath regular and deep	Lactate threshold
Zone 5	106–120 per cent	One-word answer	Aerobic capacity
Zone 6	121–150 per cent	Gasps and grunts	Anaerobic capacity
Zone 7	Greater than 150 per cent	Everything you've got	Sprint power

TABLE 1

APPS AND TOOLS (742–825)

772. I like to ride naked occasionally (that means without computers). Get back to just you and your bike. Really immerse yourself in the ride. You could call it 'mindful' cycling.

SMART TRAINERS (773–790)

773. What makes a smart trainer smart? They are basically the same as 'dumb' turbo trainers, but instead of you controlling the resistance manually, they can be hooked up to apps such as Zwift, which will control the resistance for you.

774. If you want to get the most out of virtual training and racing, these are the way to go. They make indoor cycling much more exciting and engaging.

775. Indoor training needs a lot of motivation, but smart trainers and connected apps have changed all that. With your app controlling the resistance you have something to react to and, as in real life cycling, when the road goes down on the screen the resistance eases off on your bike.

776. It's not just Zwift, smart trainers also work with rider point of view footage from apps such as Rouvy, to help you ride Alpe d'Huez in the comfort of your shed.

777. They aren't just for entertainment though. In the 'old' days a turbo interval session meant taping your session to your stem and then trying to do the maths to work out which interval you were on. With a smart trainer, you can programme in your session, and it will adjust the resistance accordingly. No more easing up before the end of the interval!

778. Most trainers work with ANT+, which is fairly universal with most cycling gadgets, and Bluetooth, which works with your smartphone if you want an app to run the smart trainer. It's pretty straightforward even for technophobes.

779. You need good Wi-Fi and a power socket – sadly the turbo that uses rider effort to power itself has not been invented yet. So, if you are still being sent out to a cold shed to use your turbo, you might have to stick with the dumb version.

780. When buying a smart trainer, you have a decision to make – wheel on or wheel off? For direct drive you mount your wheel on to the smart trainer's own cassette – it's more accurate and needs less calibration, plus it saves wrecking your rear tyre, but it's also a bit more expensive.

781. If you are going to use a smart trainer a lot and get deeply immersed in virtual cycling, it is worth getting a decent size screen at the right height. Constantly looking down at a smart phone or tablet will wreck your neck and shoulders. How long before bike fitters start offering a fit position designed for virtual racing?

782. Dumb trainers. They may be called 'dumb', but they aren't outdated. There are lots of situations where you can't hook up to power – like warming up at a race.

783. Users of dumb turbo trainers are probably getting an extra element to their training that 'smart' users aren't. It requires greater internal motivation and mental strength to do a good turbo session when you don't have an external stimulus like Zwift.

Dalila Lecky – gravel, road, cyclo-cross and track cyclist – from London, England. © Markus Stitz

784. Whatever type of turbo or roller you use, setting up your indoor training space can make a real difference. It needs to be well ventilated, ideally with a fan to keep you cool. A mat can help absorb your dripping sweat and stop the turbo rocking and making a noise.

785. For indoor training you need a lot of fluids. For long sessions and racing, dehydration is a genuine concern, as is underperformance if your core temperature starts to rise. If you want to race, invest in the best fan you can (or sit by an open door).

786. If you swap your bike between turbo training and outdoor riding, keep an eye on your back tyre as it can get squared-off by the pressure of the roller and the lack of normal side-to-side movement.

787. Sweat is highly corrosive. All those salts and electrolytes that you know you need to replace when you sweat are dripping all over your bike. Keep an eye on where sweat is pooling. Don't let your bike go rusty.

788. Don't let your skills go rusty. Turbo training is great for your fitness but bad for your technique. If you want to ride well outside and not just be a Zwift-hero then make sure you do enough IRL (in real life) riding to hone your technique.

789. Roller riding is also great for improving your balance and developing a smooth pedalling technique; it reinforces good technique as poor pedalling can result in losing your balance and falling.

790. You can listen to your turbo to assess your pedalling technique. Using a turbo trainer can allow you to get away with stamping, piston-like leg action. If you listen to the noise as you turbo and you get a 'whoosh, whoosh' noise instead of a constant hum then you are mashing down hard on one leg at a time, rather than a more even power production.

The Eastern Moors, near Sheffield, England. © *Rosie Edwards*

STRAVA (791–808)

791. Strava has been around since 2009 and is now deeply embedded in cycling culture. So much so that it is getting its own heading in this book. In 2020, 55 million people used Strava. For perspective, in 2018 the UK's population was around 66 million.

792. Like other forms of social media, Strava gives a sense of community and connection with like-minded individuals. You can plan rides, take part in challenges and keep an eye on what training your mates are doing.

793. But just remember that with the private function 'secret training' still exists. It is a lie that if it is not on Strava it didn't happen.

794. Strava serves lots of different needs; it offers mapping, training metrics and community, but it is the dopamine drip of receiving kudos on your rides and the challenge of segment chasing that makes it so addictive.

795. Thanks to Strava there are new words in the cycling lexicon: KOM and QOM (king or queen of the mountain) for those who are the fastest over a given segment. The unwieldy use of Strava as a verb, 'I'm not Stravering today', is a particularly awkward mouthful.

796. As with so many things, Strava is a great tool that can be used for good or evil. It can be a brilliant motivator and really help improve your fitness, but for some, the constant hunt for segments can border on addiction.

797. Checking out times on segments and comparing yourself to other riders can be really motivating, depending on your mindset. Picking a segment to target and watching your PR (personal record) improve and seeing yourself inch up the leader board is a good way of tracking fitness progress.

798. Strava allows virtual racing but also offers real-world performance indicators. There is a lot more to how fast you can ride a segment than just your power output. Strava gives you the opportunity to monitor improvements in your skill, technique and even aerodynamics.

799. If you are serious about your rankings on the leader board, you need to make meticulous preparations before making a KOM or QOM attempt. You need to know the exact locations of the segments and the best wind conditions to tackle them.

800. A self-confessed Strava addict, Strava Ben, as I know him, keeps a spreadsheet detailing the optimal wind direction for each segment within a route so he can cross-reference this with the weather report. It's this kind of dedication that gets you KOMs or QOMs.

801. One of the side-effects of Strava addiction is the sheer amount of time you can spend looking on the app and analysing your performance and that of your rivals. You might actually have more time for cycling without it!

802. If you are uploading to Strava even before you have taken off your cycling shoes or poured a recovery drink, you are in addiction territory.

803. If you want to discover new places to ride, the route building facility is really good, and the heat maps allow you to find popular routes, which is also good for exploring new areas.

804. When you have planned your route, you can get a fairly accurate estimated time based on your average speed, which is helpful.

805. The 'Training' section of Strava has some great products for monitoring your fitness gains and recovery needs. It's not just about virtual racing and segments. 'Fitness and Freshness' gives simple to understand and valuable information about how your training is progressing and the 'Power Curve' paints a complete picture of your strengths and weaknesses.

806. Strava has some great customised plans to follow; you won't get any specific coaching input, but they will give you some structure to stick to, and seeing your progress is very motivating.

807. Ex-pro Phil Gaimon is one of the funniest and wisest people to comment on Strava. He used the early days of his retirement from pro-racing to snap up the KOMs of known cycle cheats. His is one Strava account to definitely follow. He also holds the Everesting world record.

808. Strava segment hunting is for FUN! Stop when the fun stops.

CYCLING APPS GALORE (809–825)

809. Zwift has without a doubt changed cycling, especially competitive cycling, with virtual racing now a reality. Don't knock it until you've tried it.

810. During periods of lockdown in the Covid-19 pandemic, Zwift offered a way for cycling clubs and communities to still meet up and ride together. It's created a way for people all around the world to find like-minded people to ride with, without the worries about being dropped or having to meet strangers in bus shelters or car parks. Zwift has recorded up to 45,000 simultaneous users. It's not just for racing.

811. Zwift racing is a brilliant way to get your competitive fix any time of the day or night and without leaving the house. If you think your racing days are over, this could be the platform that proves you wrong. I know parents who race when the kids are in bed and home-workers who compete in their lunch break.

812. Zwift racing is a completely different skill set to racing in real life. There are world-class professionals getting beaten by amateurs in their garages. As with any form of cycle racing, to improve you need to look at the specific demands of the race.

813. Don't just keep your oldest and most worn out pair of shorts for indoor training – if you spend a long time riding on Zwift then the combination of sweat, training intensity and position demands a decent pair of shorts to protect your tissues from soreness.

814. The list of training apps is long and growing. The Sufferfest connects to your smart trainer and offers a complete training package with sports testing, training programmes and sessions to follow. It is performance-focused but has a supportive community to share in the highs and lows of your fitness journey. It's a great option for anyone who wants to work on developing as a cyclist.

815. If you need entertainment on your smart trainer then Rouvy is an alternative to Zwift. It's virtual, but shows real-world settings so you can tackle the iconic cols of cycling with your mates in augmented reality. It's much more visual than Zwift and feels less 'gamified'.

816. For the performance-focused, there are several key players in the data analysis and training programme sphere. TrainingPeaks and Today's Plan are two of the best. They provide analytics in a way that someone serious about their training can understand and interpret.

817. If you have the knowledge to interpret your own data, GoldenCheetah offers a range of tools for analysis, but it's best for those with coaching or scientific experience.

818. When it comes to all training data, it is knowledge and interpretation that make data meaningful. Data alone won't improve your training; it is what you do with it that counts.

819. Apps have opened up a new world of distance coaching – you can be coached by anyone, anywhere in the world, which has put professional coaching within the reach of more people. From a relatively cheap, bespoke plan to daily email contact, you can tailor the type of coaching you want to your needs, and your wallet.

820. If you really want to improve, and have the cash to spare, coaching will make more of a difference than any bit of kit you can buy.

821. Whatever you want to measure there is an app for that. From general health metrics or mood to calorie control, there isn't anything that you can't find an app for. My only advice is use them sparingly – you can easily get overwhelmed by data. The constant need to measure and tap things into your phone can make improving your health and getting fit feel like a chore.

Lunch stop in the Peak District, England. © *Rosie Edwards*

822. However, contrary to the tip above, if you struggle with motivation an app can provide a degree of accountability to your goals.

> **823.** When I'm struggling with motivation, I try streaking (again not as fun as it sounds). A streak is anything that you do daily without a break. The most famous streaker of all time is the late Ron Hill, who ran every day for 52 years and 39 days. Seeing a clean run of activity on your app makes it harder to break the pattern.

824. A really useful app to add to your phone is the St John Ambulance First Aid for Cyclists app. It's good for brushing up on your first aid knowledge and has some useful, quick tips if you need help in an emergency situation (though, obviously, your first use of your phone should be to call the emergency services, if necessary).

825. If you need help, the emergency services need to know where to find you. If you have battery and phone signal it is relatively easy to pinpoint your position or to check for yourself using an app such as what3words or OS Locate. If you don't have a working phone then being able to use a map and provide a six-figure grid reference will save a huge amount of time, which could be critical.

Naomi Freireich, three-time UK 24-hour MTB champ, pushing the last metres up the Monega Pass, Cateran Ecomusuem, Scotland.   © *Markus Stitz*

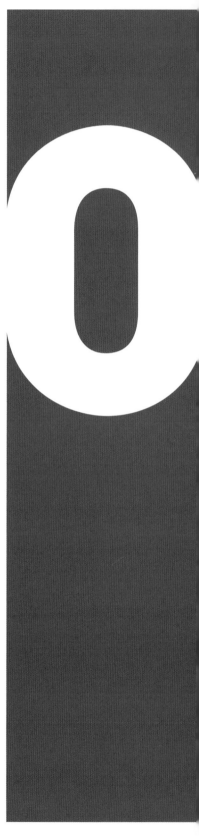

Map reading is a really useful skill for any cyclist. © *Patrick Trainor*

007

NAVIGATION AND ROUTES (826–916)

'Take a map. GPS devices are absolutely brilliant for making route planning and route following easy, but they can run out of battery, fall off your bike or lose signal.'

NAVIGATION AND ROUTES (826–916)

ROUTE-PLANNING PRINCIPLES (826–837)

826. A great bike ride starts with planning a great route. Getting lost, tired, riding further than expected or a surprise big hill at the end of the day can put even the happiest of cyclists into a grump.

827. Having said that, some of my most memorable rides and best discoveries have been down to route-planning errors!

828. Think about height gain as well as distance.

829. A flat 20-mile ride and a hilly 20-mile ride will be significantly different in terms of effort level and time taken.

830. If you have any really big climbs on your route, try to plan them into the first half of the ride when you will feel more energetic.

831. If you are planning a cafe stop, schedule it at the top of a hill not the bottom. It is no fun starting a very steep climb when you still have a full stomach!

832. Plan your shortcuts and bail-out routes in advance. I'm really good at biting off more than I can chew when it comes to route planning, so this is hard-learned advice!

833. If you have to cross busy roads, have a look at the options around. Personally, I would cycle a bit further for an easier route and safer crossing.

834. Road closures and diversions are annoying when they take you by surprise. You can look up planned road closures on local council websites and on the government-run traffic websites for England, Scotland and Wales. Most European countries also have some form of website with planned road closures on. It's always worth checking, especially when planning long routes.

835. If you hit a diversion, nine out of ten times bikes can get through, so unless there is an obvious and short route round it can be worth taking a punt that you will get through.

836. On the one out of ten times you can't get through you will curse your poor decision making and need to retrace your steps.

837. Turning back is a really difficult thing to do on a bike as it feels like wasted miles. I have variously been carried through road works in the cab of a dumper truck, shouldered my bike to wade through a stream where the bridge was out, and climbed (expensive carbon-soled shoes in hand) over a minor rock slide.

MAP READING (838–849)

838. 'You don't use a Garmin? What are you, a hippy or something?', I was once asked! Put your Garmin down occasionally, stop looking down at the purple line on your screen and explore using just a mini map in your back pocket and your brain.

839. If you don't want to carry an increasingly sweaty map with you, take a series of photos of the map on your phone.

840. Maps are art of great beauty – pore over them, learn their secrets and you will be lost in their patchwork of possibilities.

841. Watch out if the brown lines on maps are very close together – they will either make your legs hurt or your brakes squeal.

When in doubt, get the map out.   © *Hannah Reynolds*

© John Coefield

842. In the UK, riding in the direction of a black arrow marked on a road map means your brakes will squeal. They point downhill.

843. In Europe, riding in the direction of a black arrow marked on a road means your legs will hurt. They point uphill. It's a very important distinction between France and the UK!

844. If there are two black arrows close together it means your legs will really, really hurt.

845. Look for blue lines on a map – rivers are your friend. If you want a gentler ride, stick close to them, as they follow gentle gradients – just be wary of climbing in or out of steep-sided gorges!

846. Don't ride on the fat blue lines – they are motorways. You are not allowed to ride on them. Even if it's the M61 and even if you're a pro training for the Commonwealth Games. We are looking at you, Kenya's George Ochieng and Arthur Kamu.

847. The green dashes (on Ordnance Survey (OS) 1:25,000-scale maps) and pink dashes (on OS 1:50,000-scale maps) of a bridleway mean you and your bike can go there, but what you might find is highly variable, from flat field edges to rocky mountain passes. People ride their horses in pretty crazy places.

848. Don't ride on the smaller green dashes (OS 1:25,000-scale maps) or the smaller pink dashes (on OS 1:50,000-scale maps). They are footpaths, and you will get an even higher number of walkers 'tutting' at you than you will on a bridleway.

849. Try to finish your ride near a PH (public house, for the uninitiated) for vital rehydration.

NAVIGATION APPS (850–859)

850. Absolutely the easiest way to plan a route is with an app.

851. Route-planning apps includes crowd-sourced route knowledge from other cyclists to help make sure you are picking the best places to pedal.

852. Top navigation apps are Strava, Komoot, Ride with GPS and MapMyRide. There are also proprietary navigational tools on Garmin and Wahoo. They all work on similar principles, but it is worth experimenting with different ones to see what suits your needs best.

853. ViewRanger offers the depth of detail needed by off-road riders. You can purchase detailed large-scale topographical mapping for more than 10 countries. The maps are stored on your phone and use your phone's GPS location, so it doesn't need a signal or data connection to work.

854. Skyline on the ViewRanger app uses your GPS location and phone camera to help identify the peaks you are looking at. It's a nice feature for when you are sitting back and admiring the view.

855. Something to consider when choosing apps to plan a route is the level of detail you need on the finished file when following it. Garmin BaseCamp, for example, allows you to add additional information beyond just a breadcrumb trail to follow.

856. If you accidently mis-click in your route planning, the map you upload could be completely wrong! This is why you still need basic map-reading skills. See **Following a GPS route** *(tips 860–869).*

857. Busby is not strictly a navigational app but useful for when out and about on a bike. The Busby app automatically notices if you have a crash on your bike; you then have 30 seconds to respond to its question 'Are you OK?' If there is no response, your exact location, using what3words, will be sent to your listed emergency contact.

858. Navigational GPS has also given rise to the activity of dot-watching. Whether it is seeing how far from home your partner is by using Strava Beacon, or following the course of riders in events, dot-watching offers a safety aspect for riders. You may be alone but someone, somewhere, is keeping an eye on you.

859. Dot-watching allows those of us that are stuck at home or in the office to vicariously experience the thrill of long-distance routes and ultra-endurance events. It's motivating and surprisingly addictive!

FOLLOWING A GPS ROUTE (860–869)

860. If you aren't good at remembering instructions or reading maps, a GPS device takes away a lot of pressure and allows you to just focus on enjoying riding your bike.

861. But a GPS, like so many things in our modern techno-logical world, is a great tool but a poor master.

862. There are two powerful computers on your bike – your GPS device and your own brain. Your brain is the most powerful and is where responsibility lies. The problem comes when people credit the GPS with too much of its own intelligence!

NAVIGATION AND ROUTES (826-916)

863. Without looking at a map for an overview of the region you are less aware of the context of your ride and the geography of the region you are travelling through. It is easier to get disorientated if you don't have awareness of your surroundings.

864. Following the line on your GPS builds a dependency, so you stop using your own common sense. If the line takes you down a dead end, over a cliff edge or on to a motorway the danger is you just follow it without thinking 'Is this the right place for me to be riding my bike?'

> **865.** Knowing the place names or general direction of your ride can help you to avoid mindlessly following a GPS into trouble!

866. Watching the screen can remove your attention from the road and traffic when at junctions, the time you need it most. Always ride safely and if you need to check navigation pull over to the side away from traffic until you know exactly where you need to go.

867. Take a map. GPS devices are absolutely brilliant for making route planning and route following easy, but they can run out of battery, fall off your bike or lose signal.

868. When comparing routes designed and recorded on different apps, there can be huge discrepancies in altitude gain. If you and a friend do the same ride, your elevation files can be wildly different. Different apps use different algorithms to calculate elevation gains from the GPS data your computer records and every minor difference can add up over the course of a ride.

869. If you are comparing data during a ride there may be discrepancies between your computer and your mate's. Bike computers that use barometric pressure to calculate your elevation are likely to be more accurate than the one calculating it on the data track points of your route against known elevation data. At the end of the day, if you are both stood at the summit does it matter if your data is a slightly different?

WEATHER WATCHING (870-885)

870. Watch the weather or you might not have much fun riding your bike. If you can pick your time to ride you can watch the forecast and wait out the bad weather to ride in the sunshine.

871. If you can't pick your time, don't worry about the weather – just ride your bike. Weather always looks worse through the window than it does when you are out in it.

872. If you like apps, it's worth giving Epic Ride Weather a go. You input your start point, average speed and a GPX file of the route and it will tell you the weather at each point in your ride. Sometimes leaving 15 minutes later might be enough to avoid getting caught in a shower halfway round.

873. It's not just about rain – sometimes a cyclist's worst enemy is the wind. I'd pick rain over a headwind.

874. Headwinds. Plan your route to be headwind out and tailwind back. Or find a large riding mate and sit on their wheel.

> **875.** Crosswinds and gusts can be really dangerous if they take you by surprise and push you across the road. Keep an eye out when passing gaps in hedges or farm gates where the crosswind can suddenly fly through.

Ride bikes. Eat cake. No better mantra.   © *John Coefield*

NAVIGATION AND ROUTES (826–916)

876. If you're riding in the UK, wait 20 minutes and the weather will change.

877. Yes, you can get sunburnt in the UK – wear your sunscreen.

878. Pros put newspaper down their tops on long, cold descents to prevent the cold from getting to their chest. In an emergency this will do nicely.

879. Some of the best mountain bike rides can be on frozen ground as it turns wet, muddy sections into rideable routes. Just watch out for ice.

880. Hail – the cyclists' worst weather nemesis. Head for the nearest shelter and wait it out. Hailstones sting like anything.

881. Summer brings out the flowers, but it also brings out the wasps and bees. Unzipped jerseys act as a kind of funnel; if you see a cyclist frantically ripping off their clothes by the side of the road the chances are they have scooped up a stinging insect.

882. If you ride a lot in winter with your mates, make sure that you have mudguards fitted otherwise you soon won't have any mates to go riding with. No one wants a jet of cold, muddy water in the face.

883. Some cyclists are obsessed with getting up early. Ride later into the golden hour and let the soft light surround you.

884. Ride early in the morning. It's beautiful and you can feel energised (and smug) for the rest of the day.

885. When travelling, ride when the locals ride. They know the climate and temperatures best. If local culture dictates early morning riding and an afternoon siesta, there will be a good reason for it.

HILLS AND MOUNTAINS (886–905)

886. Cyclists who love mountains can be split into two categories: those who live for the climb and those who love the descent. This applies both to on-road and off-road, but is compounded off-road by the specificity of bikes designed just for the downhills.

887. Why do cyclists want to ride up mountains? The easiest answer can be given in the words of George Mallory when asked why he wanted to climb Everest: 'Because it's there.' When a cyclist sees a sinuous, thin strip of tarmac, or hazy gravel track, snaking its way up to a cloud-shrouded peak, the urge is to follow it.

888. Mallory had a longer answer to why he wanted to climb Everest, but the essence of it is there in every cyclist tackling their own, albeit more minor, mountain. When we climb a mountain, when we sweat and toil, and dig deep in our legs and mind, the sensation at the top is euphoric. Mallory expressed it as, 'If you cannot understand that there is something in man which responds to the challenge of this mountain and goes out to meet it, that the struggle is the struggle of life itself upward and forever upward, then you won't see why we go. What we get from this adventure is just sheer joy. And joy is, after all, the end of life. We do not live to eat and make money. We eat and make money to be able to live.' And that is why cyclists climb mountains, to feel alive.

889. It is also why road cyclists and mountain bikers descend mountains. Nothing beats the adrenaline rush and feeling of flying you get from a long descent.

890. Climbs are an indispensable part of a great route. Whereas in life you need lows to appreciate the highs, in cycling it is reversed. It is from the suffering of the climb that you win the descent.

891. I challenge anyone to get to the top of a mountain, whether that be by pedal power, ebike motor or cable car, and not feel the thrill of high places.

892. Just looking at mountain-scapes raises my heart rate. Baking hot sun on your neck and sweat dripping off your nose on to your stem as you inch and haul your bike up a pedal stroke at a time. Then, at the top, the glorious release of a fast, swooping downhill, just the sound of your free wheel and wind rushing past your ears as you and your bike flow sinuously around every curve.

893. However well you know a climb, treat it with respect. The day we become arrogant enough to believe climbing is easy is the day we forget to drink or eat enough. A lack of care for the challenge leads to blowing up – reaching the summit at a crawl, a spent and humbled rider.

894. Descending on a road bike needs skill and a healthy balance between letting go and caution.

895. Excessive use of rim brakes on long descents can lead to a build-up of heat in the rims from the friction which can result in tyre blowouts. Make sure you brake and release to control your speed rather than drag your brakes against the rim throughout the whole descent.

896. Disc brakes also heat up on descents; you might even hear the telltale 'ping' of your rotors cooling down when you stop. Be very careful not to touch a hot disc brake or lean against it – rotor burns on your calves are not cool.

897. Do not underestimate the importance of descending when it comes to road competition. It is a skill that needs practice. Over a long descent you can save seconds, even minutes, over rivals by descending fast, but safely.

898. If you can feel relaxed, confident and in control on descents it will feel much less tiring. You will be able to use the descent for recovery rather than finding it exhausting. It doesn't take any extra fitness to be good at descending and it is an often overlooked part of competitive cycling which everyone can turn to their advantage.

899. When it comes to mountain biking, descents are a huge part of the fun, thrill and culture of the sport. You can still love off-road cycling without being brilliant on the descents, but you are missing out. Learning some trail skills, preferably with someone who can coach good technique, can transform your riding.

900. On easy, off-road descents the three key things to remember are: head up, weight back and heels down.

901. *Head up*, so you are scanning the trail ahead, ready to adjust your line or speed.

902. *Weight back* and bottom off the saddle to counteract gravity and stop yourself tipping forward over the handlebars, and to maintain some grip at your rear wheel. With your bottom up and your knees bent your legs act as natural shock absorbers and your bike is free to move around underneath you.

903. *Heels down* – pushing your bike into the ground puts you in a strong, balanced position and keeps your tyres gripping.

904. Dropper posts are one of the greatest innovations of mountain biking. They drop the saddle down and out of your way, allowing you to move your body around the bike and get your weight back with much more ease. It is hilarious to look at 1990s mountain bike photos and see the downhill stance of the riders with their chests almost on the saddle.

Cycling the dusty dirt roads of Myanmar. © *Hannah Reynolds*

905. Remember to put your dropper post back up for the climbs!

LONG-DISTANCE ROUTES (906–916)

906. Where are you going? What's the aim? Maybe you have no idea on either of these questions. No problem, just wander and enjoy. Don't be scared of unplanned journeys, they can often be the most rewarding.

907. Cycle from Land's Ends to John o' Groats at least once in your life. Yes, the UK is wet, but it also has some amazing and varied riding. I'd also argue that you can experience as much, if not more, cultural change, from accents to food, in 1,000 miles across the UK than 1,000 miles nearly anywhere else in the world. Take the LEJOG 1000 – the ultimate journey across Britain – to follow the most interesting of routes.

908. Don't follow the main roads. Take the *chemin des écoliers*, the winding road a school kid takes to avoid getting to school too early. When it comes to cycle touring it really is the journey, not the destination, that defines the experience.

909. Planning long-distance point-to-point journeys is a balance between finding the most interesting way, and actually covering enough ground per day. It's a constant tug of war between these demands. Sometimes you might need a bit of boring busy road to help you get there, so try to offset it with something more interesting and beautiful.

910. Aim for each day to take the same length of time rather than to be the same distance. Make hillier days shorter in distance than flat days.

911. A shorter, flatter day makes a good easy day mid trip, but keeps you moving along.

912. On long trips, a complete day off can be beneficial, but weirdly your legs can suffer from the lack of riding and feel heavy the next day. My preference is to enjoy the rest that staying two nights in the same place gives, but still do a light ride of an hour or so to keep my legs in good condition.

913. Try to avoid a long ride on the day of departure, particularly if you need to catch a train, plane or boat. It is tempting to maximise your riding and distance, but it can become incredibly stressful if you have a mechanical or make a navigational error when there is no time to spare. And expensive when you miss your plane. It's not a mistake you make twice.

914. Route planning for multi-day trips is always a compromise between how far you want to ride and where the good places to stop are. Unfortunately, they don't build amazingly good, budget hotels with hot tubs and bike storage at exact intervals where you would like them to be for your journey. Sometimes you may need to pedal a bit longer to find them.

915. Who needs a hotel? Try wild camping, then you can stop whenever you want!

916. Unless you are going for a timed record, allow yourself some flexibility each day to deviate from your planned route. The pleasure of a tour is having the freedom to stop at places that rouse your curiosity or to follow interesting deviations; don't deprive yourself of this to stick to a precise itinerary.

Enjoying riding between the vines of the Champagne region of France.   © *John Walsh*

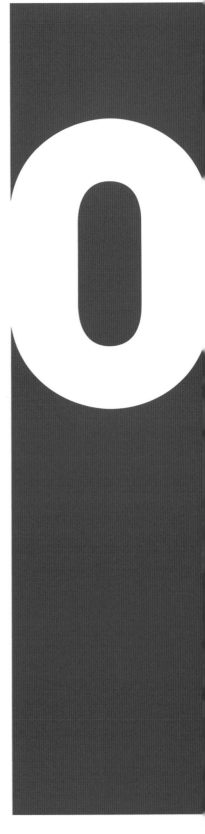

Sarah Ross and Richard Ross on the North Coast 500, Scotland. © *Stephen Ross*

008

TRAVELLING BY BIKE (917–992)

*'Wearing clean shorts every day of your trip is essential
— it is the most important step in avoiding the dreaded
saddle sores!'*

Travel writer Simon Parker on the ever-changing field on the John Muir Way near North Berwick, Scotland. © *Markus Stitz*

TRAVELLING BY BIKE (917-992)

ESSENTIAL KIT ON TOURS (917-928)

917. Some items are universal on cycling tours, whether you are living it up in hotels every night or bivvying down in the woods. Get the basics right and everything else is easier.

> **918.** Nothing feels better if you have got wet or cold than putting on clean, dry socks. It barely matters what the rest of you is wearing as long as you have fresh socks on.

919. Whether it is to drown out the snoring of your room-mate, cut out the laughter from the bar below or silence the cicadas when they are making a racket, a set of earplugs can make a real difference to your night's sleep when you are staying somewhere unfamiliar.

920. Separate bags are the easiest way to avoid kit bag explosions! Put your daily cycling kit in one, your wet or cold weather cycling gear in a separate one and your off-the-bike casual clothes in another. This way you can easily grab the items you need without having to pull everything out of your bag.

921. Wearing clean shorts every day of your trip is essential – it is the most important step in avoiding the dreaded saddle sores!

922. When packing for a trip, the best plan is a minimum of two pairs of shorts so you can alternate them just in case they don't fully dry out overnight.

923. Drying your shorts chamois pad outwards in direct sunshine can help to kill bacteria, but be sensitive about where you hang up your undergarments!

> **924.** If your trip includes visits to temples, churches or anywhere there is a dress code, make sure you have something that you can slip over your cycling kit to cover your legs and shoulders.

925. Trying new foods is part of the fun of travel, but some people find it comforting to have a few familiar snacks, especially if riding all day, so throw in a couple of treats.

926. If you are decanting toiletries into smaller pots make sure they are clearly labelled so the right creams go in the right places.

927. A notebook is a really quick and easy way to jot down the things you notice and the thoughts you have as you travel. Some of the notebooks I have kept are impregnated with smells and marks which speak of where I have been and remind me of specific places. You don't get this jotting down notes on your phone.

928. Keep a diary of the boring bits. I read a great piece of advice in a book called *The Gentle Art of Tramping*. The author, Stephen Graham, suggests keeping notes of the day-to-day because, he argues, you will naturally remember the big and spectacular things, but it is the mundane details that will slip away. These are very wise words as it is the mundane things that often make up the complete fabric of a trip.

CAMPING AND FOOD (929-940)

929. If you know you will be able to buy food en route, don't carry more than you need for the next day.

930. Do have an emergency, lightweight food stash for those days when you forget the shops will be shut or there is a religious celebration or bank holiday you didn't know about.

TRAVELLING BY BIKE (917–992)

931. Hot food and hot drinks are as much about comfort as nutrition, but you can survive, and even enjoy, a tour without taking cooking apparatus, especially if you are somewhere with plenty of cafes and restaurants.

932. If you fill a metal bottle or flask with hot water before bed, it will make a good hot water bottle and be just warm enough for a tea or instant coffee in the morning, so you can get going without lighting the stove.

933. Don't buy tins that need tin openers. Yes, there is a tin opener on a Swiss army knife, but it always takes ages and if you are as clumsy as me you will end up cutting your hand.

934. If you can't live without coffee then by all means take a fancy drip filter or AeroPress but remember, if you are in most European countries and not far off the beaten track, you will be able to get a decent coffee in a village at any time of day for a very reasonable price.

935. Sharing the coffee ritual in a local cafe, regardless of the quality of the coffee, is a great way to people watch. And no doubt with your bike and cycling outfit there will be plenty of people who want to chat to you too.

936. Paint your tent pegs so you can find them more easily in the grass.

937. If you are worried about security overnight, tie your bike to your wrist or your tent pole. If anyone tugs on it, you will wake up. (I have no advice on what to do next, I never thought about that when I was camping.)

938. Develop a system for unpacking and packing your bike. Try to always put things in the same place — it's quicker and you are less likely to lose things.

939. Double and triple check before you leave a site. Riding 15 kilometres back the way you have come for something you have forgotten is demoralising.

940. If you have a foam mat to sleep on, cut it down to your exact length. They are bulky and take up a lot of space.

CREDIT CARD TOURING (941–950)

941. Credit card touring is the most civilised way of travelling by bike. Sweat and toil in the day and luxury at night.

942. Attitudes to cyclists arriving at a hotel vary depending on the country. The UK is amongst the worst. Hotel and B&B owners who see you turn up on a bike frequently assume that you are travelling on the cheap, will leave a mess and steal all the breakfast buffet. They often give you the worst rooms and are reluctant to help with secure bike storage. In France, where cycling is part of the culture and it is understood that people travel by bike because they want to, not because they have to, the response is very different. One hotelier in Châteauneuf-du-Pape tenderly tucked my bike up in his cellar amongst his finest vintages.

943. If you are worried by the reception you might get then make sure you book ahead by phone or email. It is easy for an owner to make the excuse they are full if they don't like the look of you, but harder for them to turn away a pre-paid booking.

944. If you haven't booked all your accommodation ahead don't leave it too late in the day to find your night's stay. Looking for somewhere with vacancies, and feeling the pressure as the night draws on, is exhausting.

Rolling over Stanage Edge in the Peak District, England. © *John Coefield*

Canal towpaths make great car-free cycle routes. © *Joolze Dymond*

TRAVELLING BY BIKE (917–992)

945. You don't have to always rely on the internet for your bookings. Most towns and many small villages in Europe have some form of tourist information centre. The staff will be able to make suggestions, phone places for you and know of places to stay that may not even appear online.

946. In places without a tourist information centre, the obvious place to head to is a bar or cafe. If there isn't any accommodation left in town you may get lucky (or unlucky) with the bar owner or a patron of the bar offering you a bed.

947. In my experience, I don't feel self-conscious about my cycling clothes when I am with my bike, because it is obvious that I am cycling, but I do feel uncomfortable in a bar or hotel restaurant in an evening. I prefer to pack one decent evening outfit and pair of lightweight sandals so that I do not look like an off-duty cyclist.

948. Cycling clothing brands are making more kit aimed at touring cyclists that looks acceptable off the bike and performs well on it. Investing in a few pieces of kit could save on packing space and washing.

949. One of the advantages of credit card touring is that you can wash and dry kit every night, saving on the amount of clothing you need. I'm OK with wearing slightly damp kit if it hasn't dried overnight, but nothing beats fresh socks, so this is where I splash out and I carry three pairs.

950. Even with the luxury of indoor electricity, you may struggle to keep everything charged. A dual USB port plug is really handy for making the most of every available socket. Or charge a power pack that can hold enough energy for multiple devices.

KIT BAG PACKING (951–962)

951. If you are having your kit carried for you, you have the luxury of carrying as much as you want. But just remember that after a day of cycling a bag that felt light at home will feel significantly heavier.

952. On a long cycling trip or stage race you may end each day completely knackered. Overpacking or disorganised packing means more decisions and makes it harder to find things. Pack for your tired, confused future self.

953. Choose a kit bag wisely, especially if you travel a lot. I prefer the soft duffle bag style that can also be worn as a rucksack. With your bag on your back you have a spare hand for wheeling your bike or bike bag.

954. Dry bags – fully sealed, waterproof bags – are really useful for dirty, sweaty kit as they keep the stench in. Just be prepared to stand well back when opening them when you get home.

955. Colour-coded mesh bags are perfect for clean clothes and other items, and you can see what is in them without undoing the zip.

956. I keep one bag for next-to-skin layers: socks, shorts and vests, which will be the same regardless of the layers you put on over the top.

957. Another bag has jerseys and outer layers.

958. An additional bag is needed for accessories such as arm and knee warmers, scarves, hats and so on.

959. Another bag has everything you need for rainy days, from overshoes to a rain jacket.

960. Finally, you also need a 'civvies' bag – a quick-to-access bag of non-cycling kit because when you get off your bike you'll want to get out of your sweaty kit as quickly as possible.

961. On numerous stage races or cycling tours I have had the misfortune of sharing rooms with a kit-bag rustler. For some people, shuffling their kit around is a way of dealing with nerves, but it is really annoying, and it reduces the rest time of both the person doing the shuffling and their room-mate.

962. Get into a routine as quickly as possible. At the end of each day put your helmet, glasses and shoes in the same place. Put electronics on to charge early. Lay out your kit for the following day well before you go to bed, so you aren't making decisions or looking for things when you're tired. The more things you can build into your routine, the less you need to think about.

PANNIER PACKING (963–972)

963. When you haven't got much, everything needs to have a purpose, preferably more than one!

964. Use dry bags, ideally colour coded, both to split up your kit and so that you know what is in each one.

965. Keep things you might need in the day near the top of the panniers and things you only need at camp right at the bottom.

966. Pack things in the same order every time so you never waste time looking for things.

967. Use an elastic band, wedge or clip to hold your brakes on while you load your panniers on to the rack to stop the bike rolling away!

968. Pack a small bag with your most vital and important valuables at the top of your panniers so you can pull it out and carry it with you anytime you leave your bike for more than a few seconds.

969. Bungee cords are really useful for securing extra things to the top of your panniers temporarily, such as food shopping. They also make a good washing line.

970. On a long tour, occasional loop rides without your panniers will remind you of how cycling feels unencumbered. You will feel like you are flying! It's good for the head and the legs.

971. Tourist information centres and bike shops are good places to leave your panniers securely for a few hours.

972. Everyone has one little luxury that makes their day feel special or touring a little bit easier. You don't have to sacrifice everything to save weight, just weigh up whether it is worth the effort of carrying it.

BIKEPACKING PACKING (973–981)

973. Bikepacking as a concept works better for tall people. Their bikes are much bigger and have more room for bags.

974. Any bike can work for bikepacking as you don't *need* eyelets or rack mounts. Whatever bike you ride, you can go bikepacking on it.

975. Balance out where you place bags on your frame, so you don't disrupt the overall handling of your bike too much.

976. Weight matters even more when you get off-road. The less you carry the more you will enjoy the riding time. But this means sacrifices in comfort when you get off the bike.

977. Buy the best sleeping bag you can afford. Down is great because it is really warm, light and packs up small, just don't let it get wet.

978. A light and thin insulated jacket is essential. Make sure it is thin enough to wear it on the bike in really bad conditions.

979. Put your insulated jacket in your sleeping bag stuff sack for an instant pillow or on really cold nights wear it in bed!

980. Shoving your next day's clothes down at the bottom of your sleeping bag means you can get dressed in the morning without getting out of your bag and everything stays dry and warm.

981. Changing your shorts every day and sleeping in something loose on your lower body are essential for preventing saddle sores, but you can get away with sleeping in the base layers you are riding in on your upper body if you are feeling particularly lazy or exhausted.

LIFE ON THE ROAD (982–992)

982. Culture is different everywhere we travel. It is easy to think we only experience cultural changes when we step off a long-haul flight, but that's not true if you are alive to and curious about the subtle differences of the places you pass through.

983. If you ever get sick of your friends mocking your Lycra, or of car drivers' close passes, or reading hate-fuelled comments about cycling on social media, then go to France. France is the spiritual home of cycling – the pneumatic tyre was invented here, and it is home to the greatest cycling race in the world. It will renew your love of cycling – plus the scenery, roads, food and wine are all pretty good too!

Sarah Ross starts the Hebridean Way on Barra, Outer Hebrides. © *Stephen Ross*

Enjoying an autumnal ride along the canal near Saltaire, West Yorkshire, England. © *Joolze Dymond*

TRAVELLING BY BIKE (917–992)

984. Few people want to be offensive when travelling, but it can be done inadvertently by not knowing the finer details of cultural etiquette. Learning a little before you travel helps but, more importantly, listening, observing and asking questions when you arrive will give you the greatest sensitivity to local culture.

985. Two of the best things you can bring on your holiday are open eyes and an open mind. Observation, curiosity and a willingness to give everything a go will lead you to the most fascinating and exciting discoveries.

986. Trust the people you meet. It is often difficult to trust strangers when we might spend most of our lives in an urban culture where people tend to 'keep themselves to them-selves', but when travelling with your bike, especially solo, interactions with strangers are vital. Whether it is finding a bed for the night, getting help with a problem, or a chat about your journey, these conversations are the lifeblood of travelling and can renew your belief in human nature.

987. Take the cherries. I was riding up a long mountain pass on my own just as it was getting dark. From the valley below, I heard the distinctive sound of car being driven fast, the pounding of a bass speaker accompanying the slamming of the gears and squealing of tyres in and out of every hairpin turn. As it drew nearer, I became acutely aware of being a small, blonde, lone female on a bike. The boy racer in his souped-up car sped past me, then screeched to a halt in a lay-by just ahead of the next bend. I saw him get out of his car, get some-thing then start walking down the road toward me. With a racing heart, I kept pedalling, intent on just getting past him. Slowly his beaming smile came into focus, he was holding out a box of fresh cherries: 'Bon courage, mademoiselle, these are for you.' Finding the balance between self-protection and openness to experience takes time to get used to, but when someone with a smile offers cherries, take them.

988. Local people will have established set patterns for eating because they know what works in their climate, and the best way to enjoy it is to join in. In hot countries, the locals often have a very light breakfast then a long, heavy lunch, followed by a good sleep in the shade when it is too hot to do anything else.

989. Hunger is the best sauce, and, like an army, cyclists travel on their stomachs. Sitting in a restaurant is always pleasant, but the most memorable meals are often the spontaneous ones, when you pull up to a cafe, or grab a snack from a street vendor, and eat your meal with strangers taking a break in their own day.

990. Even if you haven't done as much cycling preparation as you wanted (and no one ever does) you will be able to 'ride yourself into fitness' during your trip. You will be exercising more than you are used to, but you will also have more time to relax and recover at the end of the day. With nothing more arduous to do than wash your cycling shorts, you can happily put your feet up and let your tired legs rebuild, ready for the next day's challenge.

991. A super-quick technique to wash your shorts on the road is to jump in the shower still wearing your kit. Lather up some soap and rub it over the outside of your kit before stripping it off and lathering the inside paying particular attention to the pad inside your shorts. Wash yourself and let the soap you have used rinse through your garments and then give them an extra good rinse with the shower head. Gently wring out the water and stick them in the sink to drain.

992. To dry your kit, lay out the bath towel on the floor and arrange all your kit on it. Roll the towel up and then walk up and down on it so you are pressing the water out of your clothes into the towel. Think of it as treading grapes!

You will never regret a bike ride. Particularly with a classic climb like Mam Nick in the Peak District, England. © *John Coefield*

Tranquil riverside cycling in Myanmar.   © Hannah Reynolds

009

EVERYTHING ELSE
(993–1001)

'You will never regret a bike ride.'

Louise Chavarie tackling the dusty gravel trails in the Lomond Hills, Fife, Scotland. © *Markus Stitz*

EVERYTHING ELSE (993–1001)

FINAL THOUGHTS (993–1001)

993. Cycling is a way of life, not just a sport or hobby.

994. Too many bike riders get caught up in the cliques and identities of being a certain type of bike rider. Don't limit yourself.

995. Who you wave to on a bike has become a bit of a thing. In some ways it is symptomatic of the growing number of people on bikes. You don't say 'good morning' to everyone in your tube carriage, but you might to the three or four people you see walking down the street in your village. In my experience the fewer bike riders you see the more likely you are to say hello to each other.

996. But if you are going to say hello or wave to other riders, don't make distinctions based on whether they are riding fat tyres or thin, wear their socks above or below their knee warmers, or wear Lycra or baggies.

997. Cycling is a sport for every phase of your life. In just my own experience of cycling, I have raced, toured, ridden my bike to the shops and towed my son in a trailer.

998. If you start to feel jaded by the cycling you do, try something different. Switching it around keeps things fresh, teaches new skills and broadens your social circle.

999. If you feel good, ride a bike.

1000. If you feel bad, a ride will make you feel better.

1001. You will never regret a bike ride.

Cyclists on Barra, Outer Hebrides.   © *Stephen Ross*

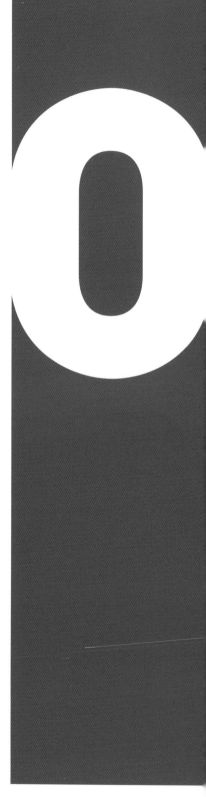

Cycling is a sport for every phase of your life.   © John Coefield